PRESCOTT BURR'S
TATTOO SKETCHES STENCILS & OUTLINES

Prescott Burr's Tattoo Sketches Stencils and Outlines
Author Prescott Burr

Publisher: Religion Mister Kind and Generous
Language: English
Country: United States
ISBN ID: 13066327
ISBN: 978-1-105-99935-2

Hi There,

The following is a book of tattoo drawings
I have done over sometime. The drawings
themselves have been appropriated from
various sources, and conveniently complied
to serve your needs.

This book can be used as a source of
inspiration for a new tattoo, or as a nice
resource book for any artist.

These drawings can be used as references
for your own drawings, or photocopied and
stenciled.

I hope this book finds you well, and your
purchase proves helpful, useful or at least
a nice addition to your library.

All the best!

Prescott Burr

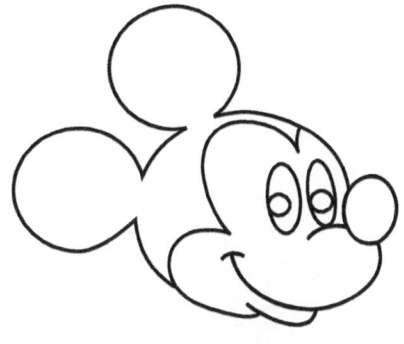

"Americana"

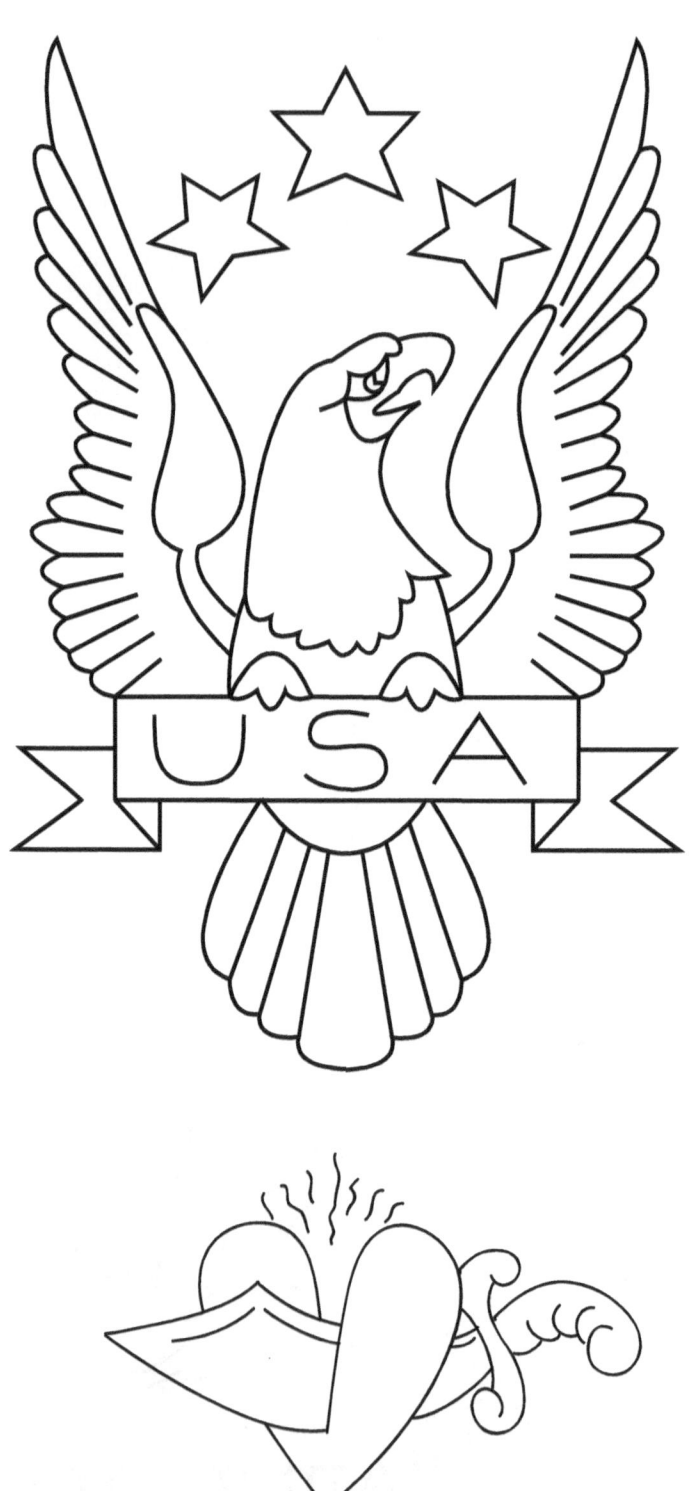

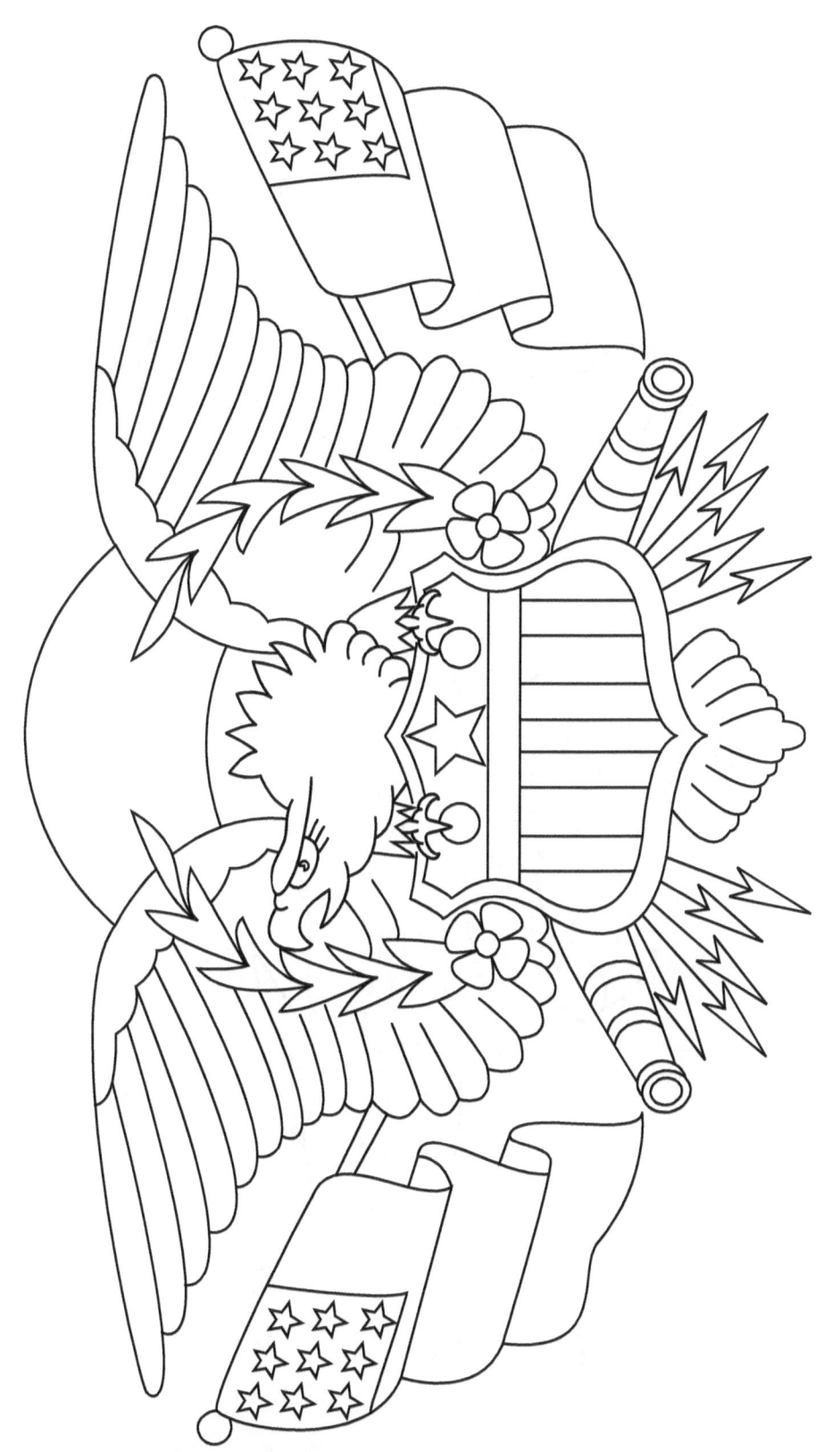

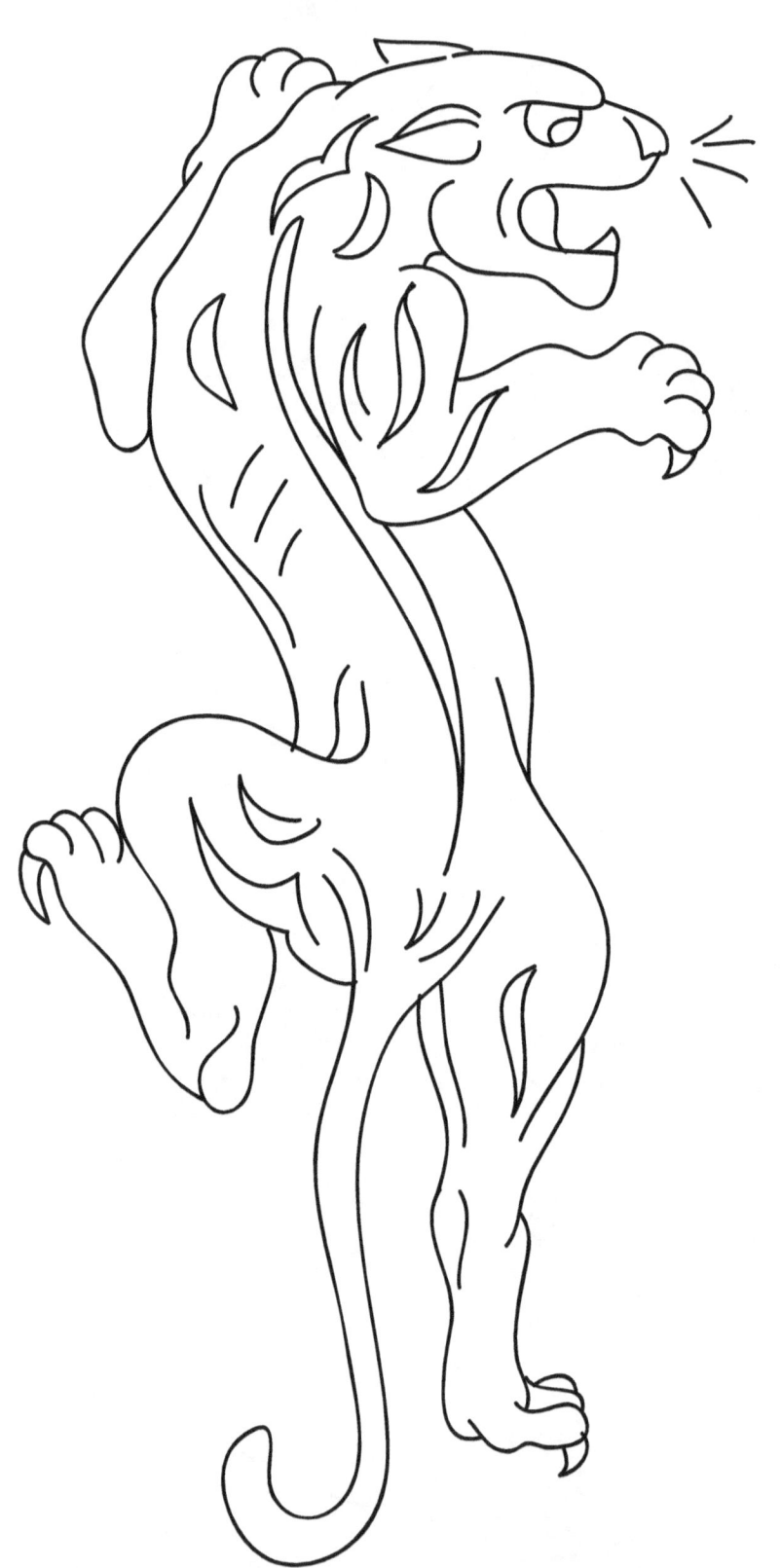

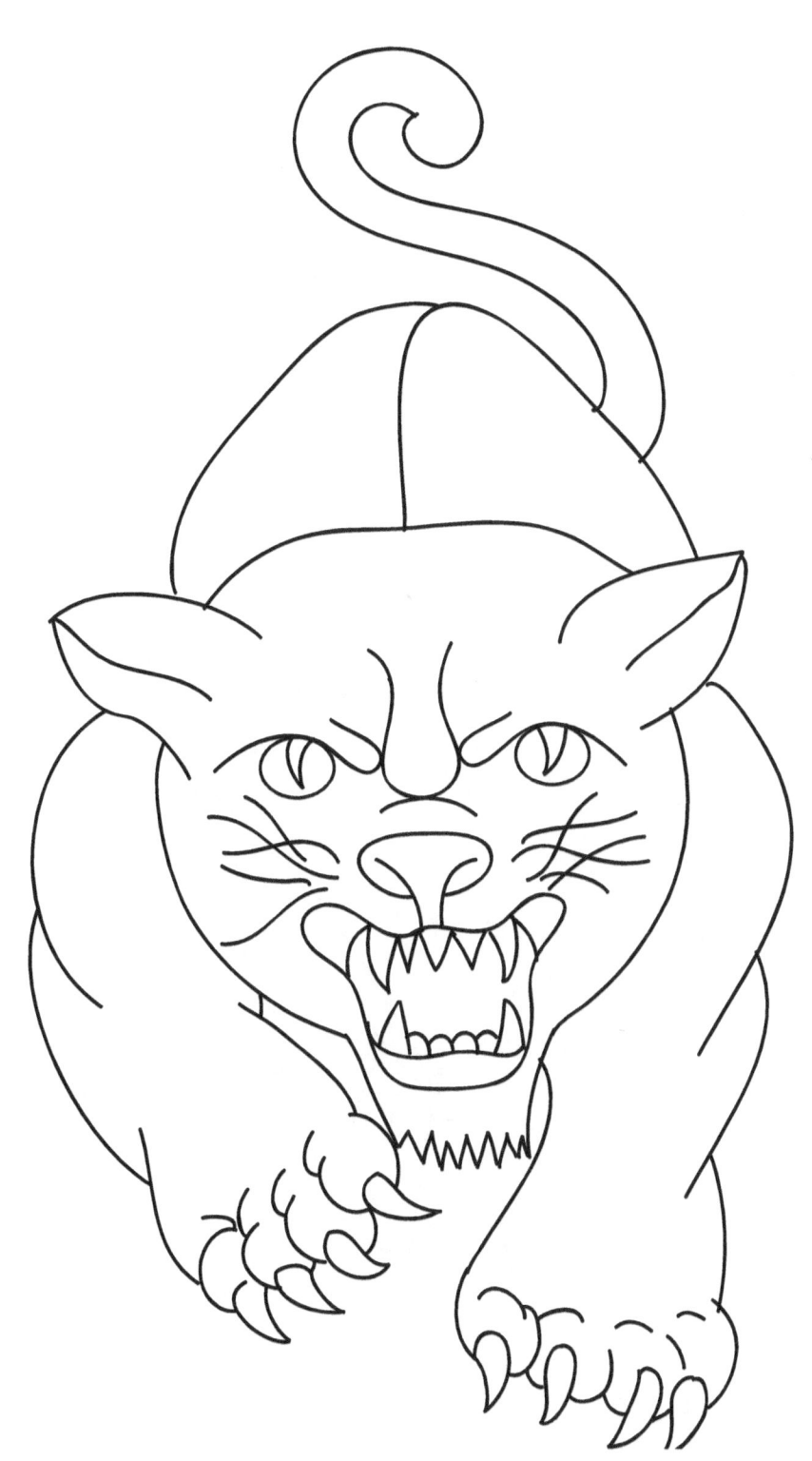

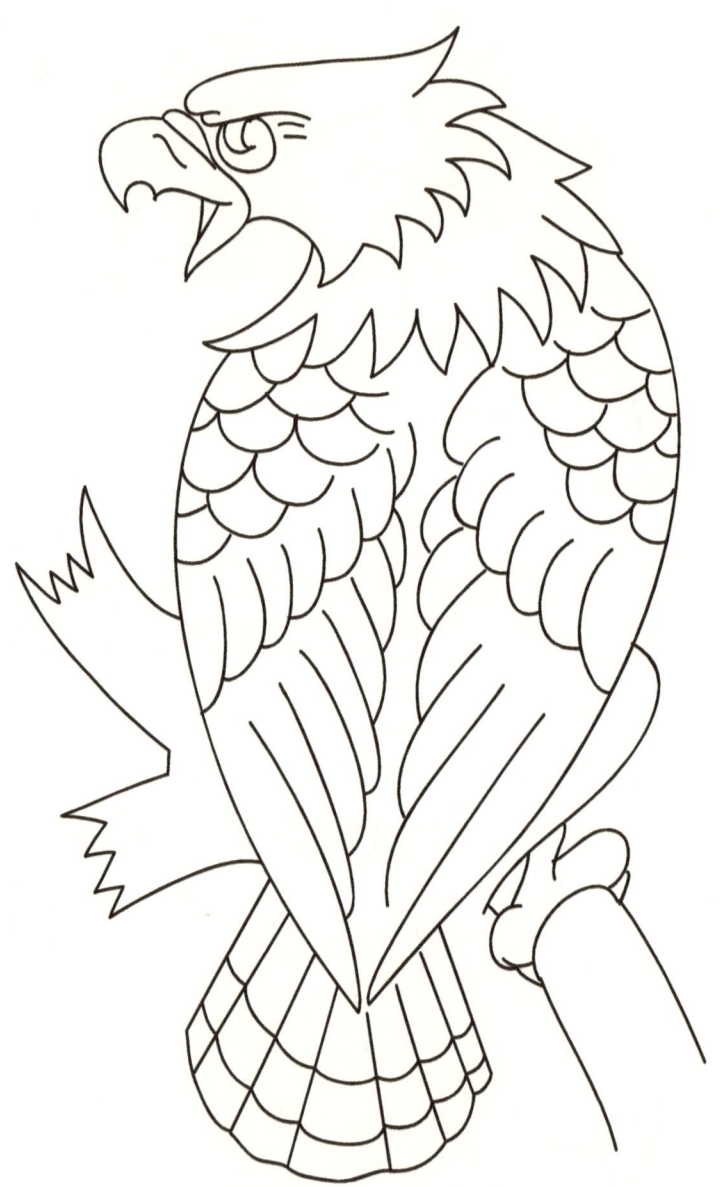

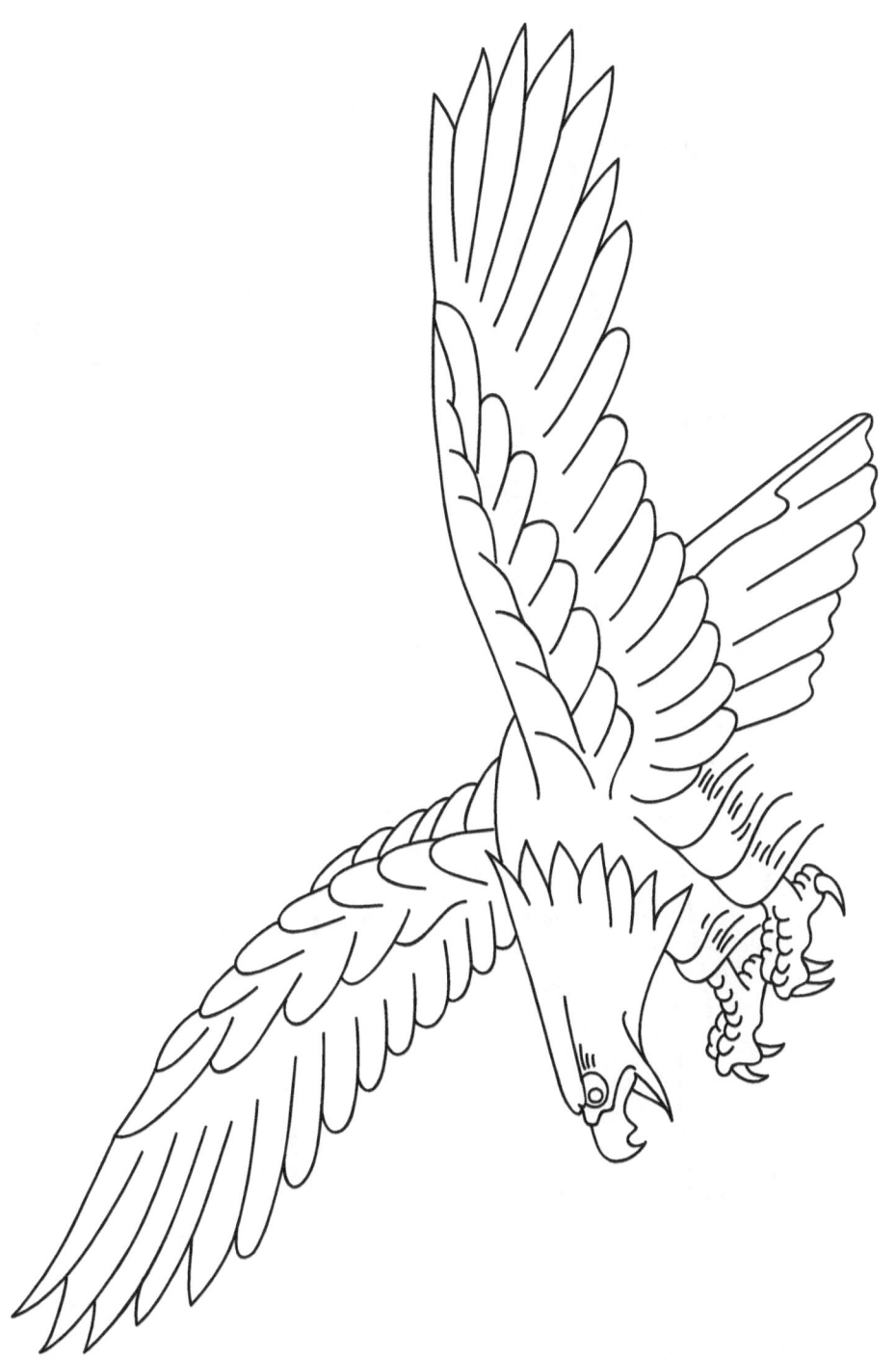

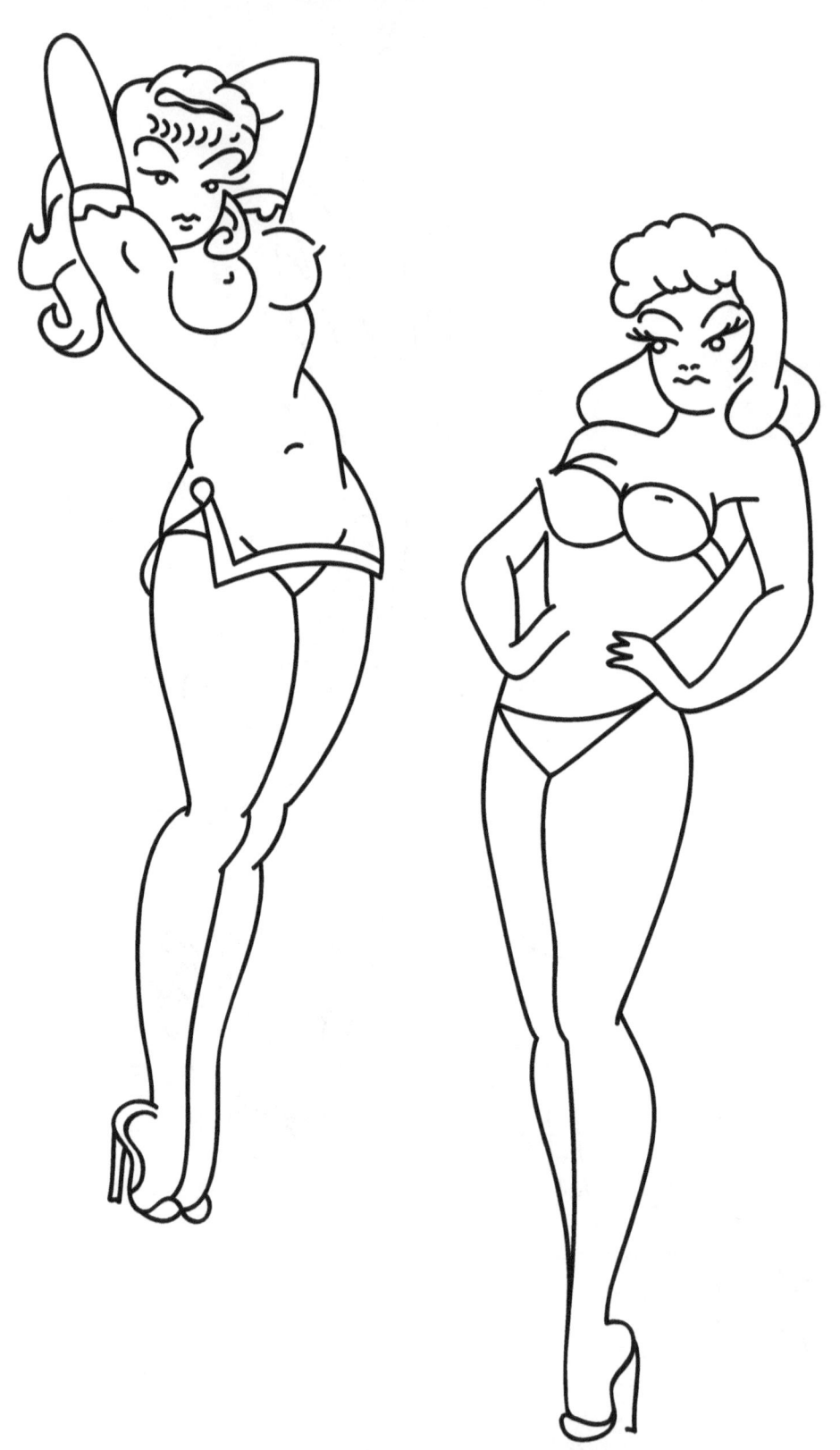

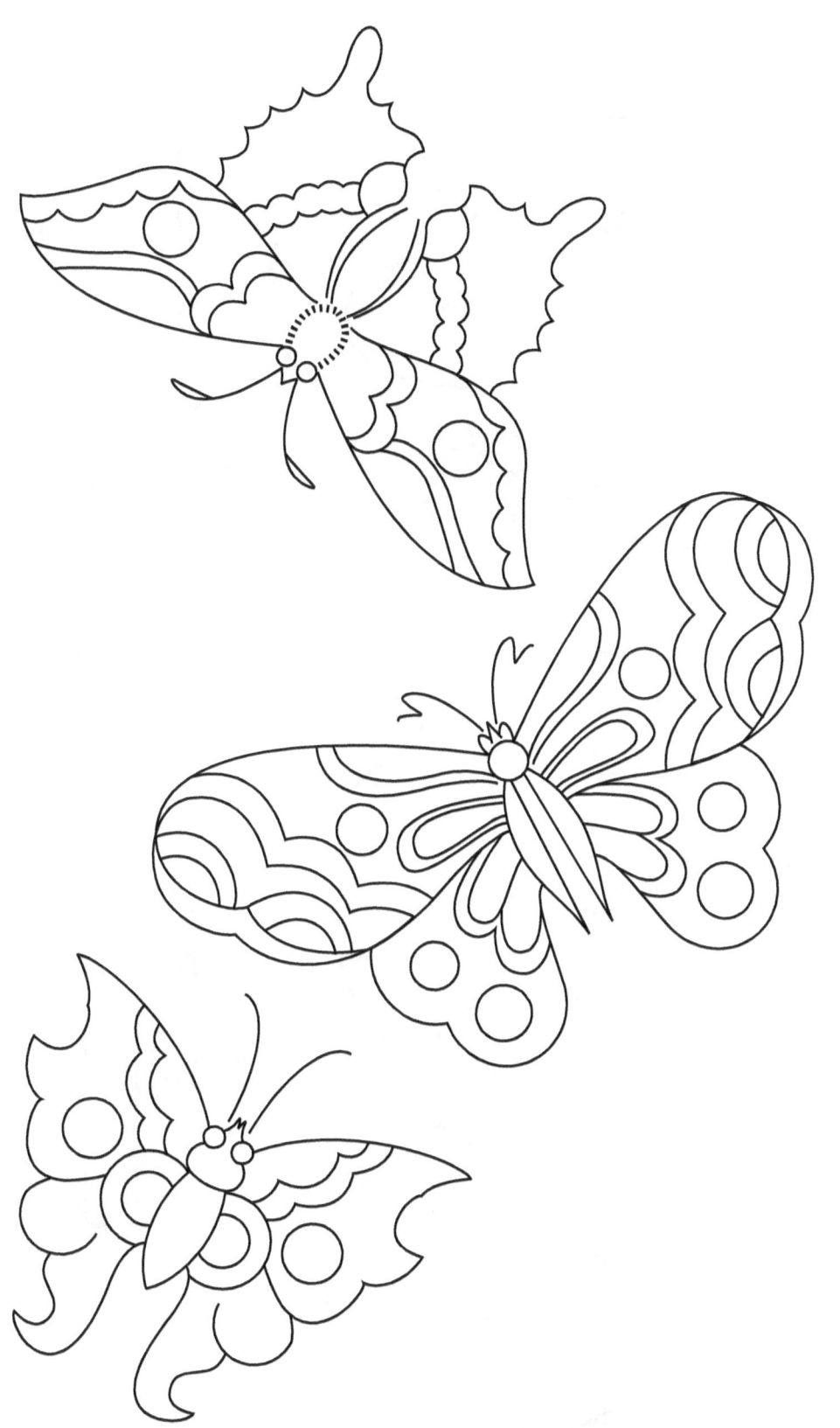

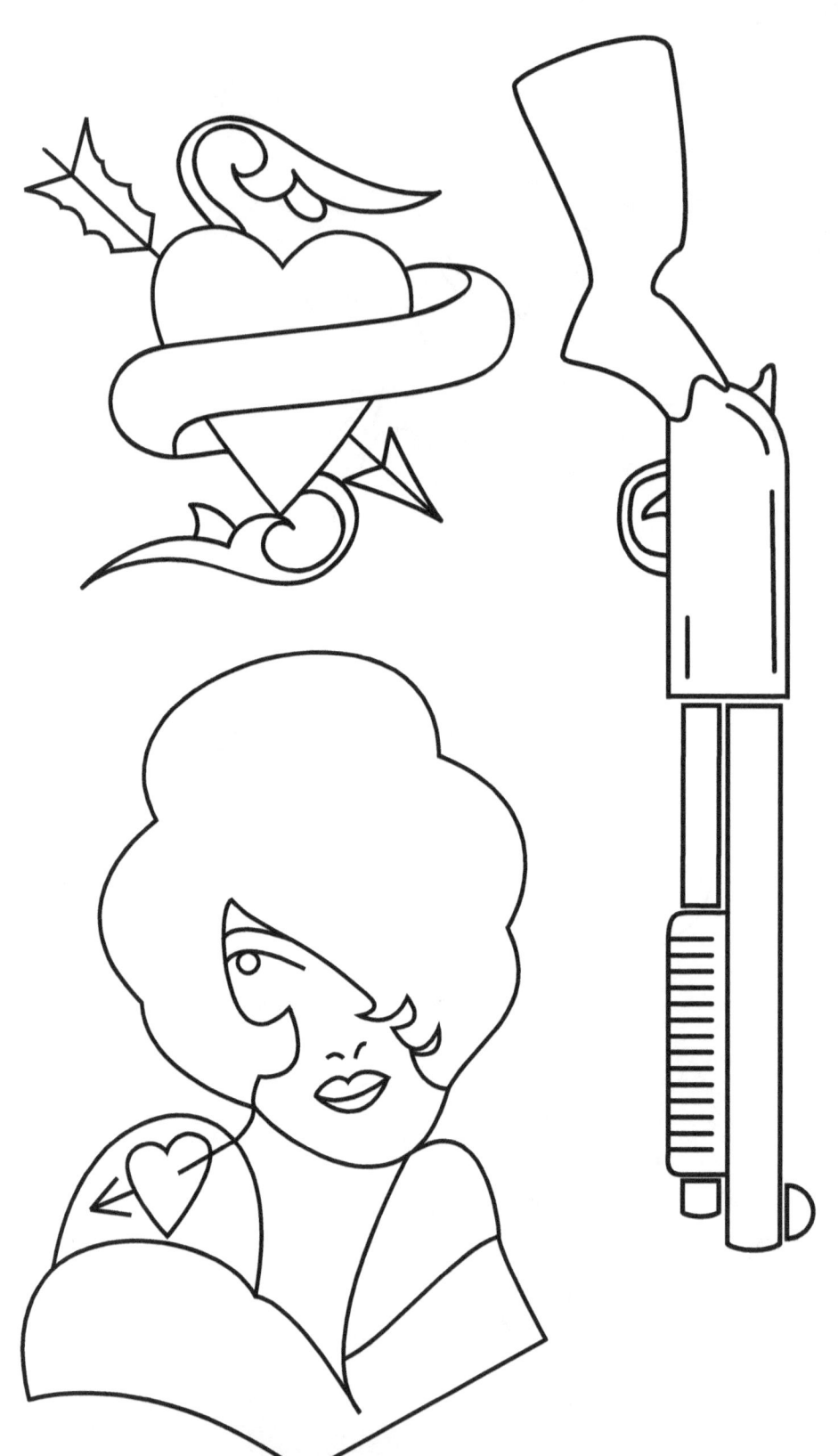

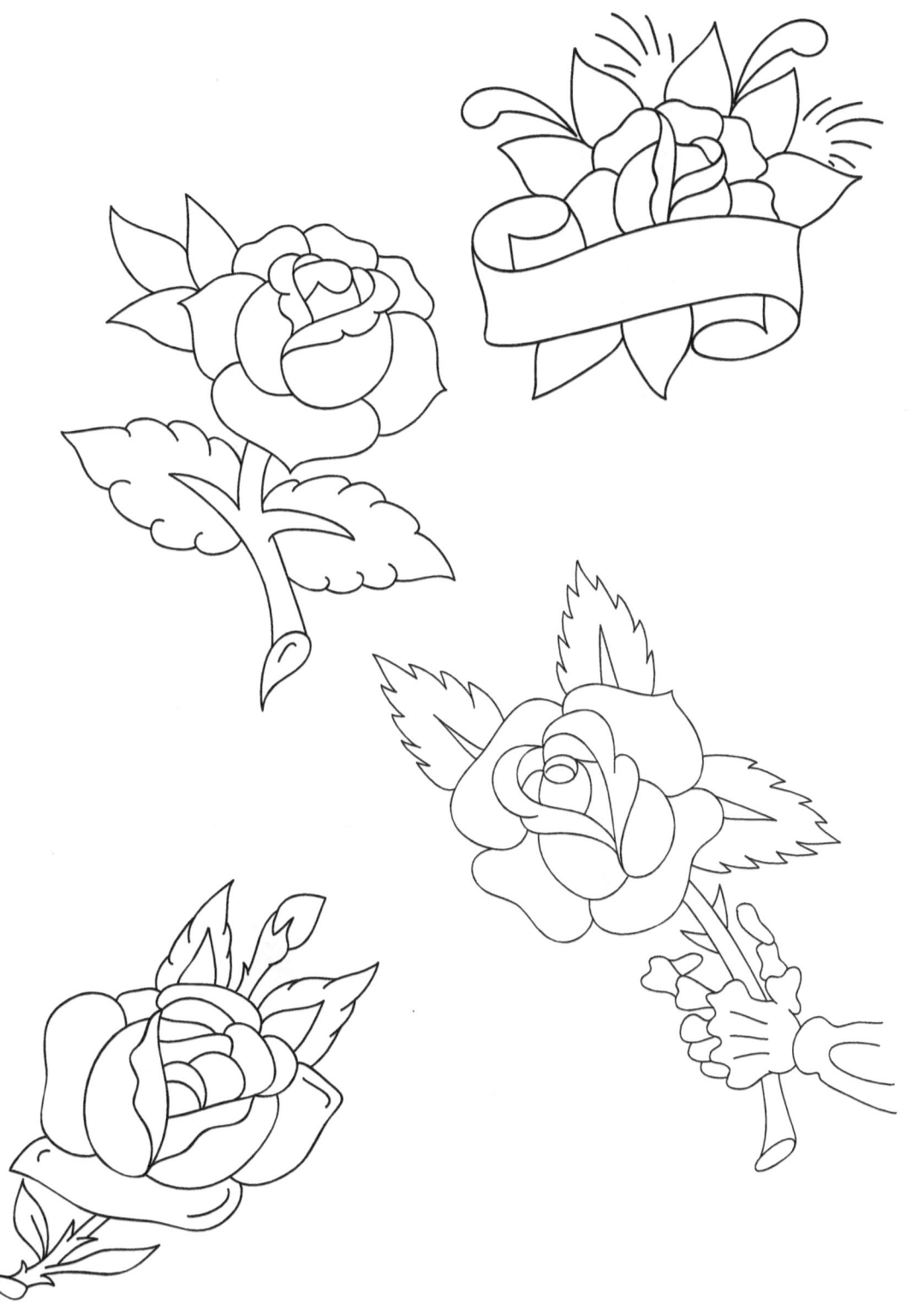

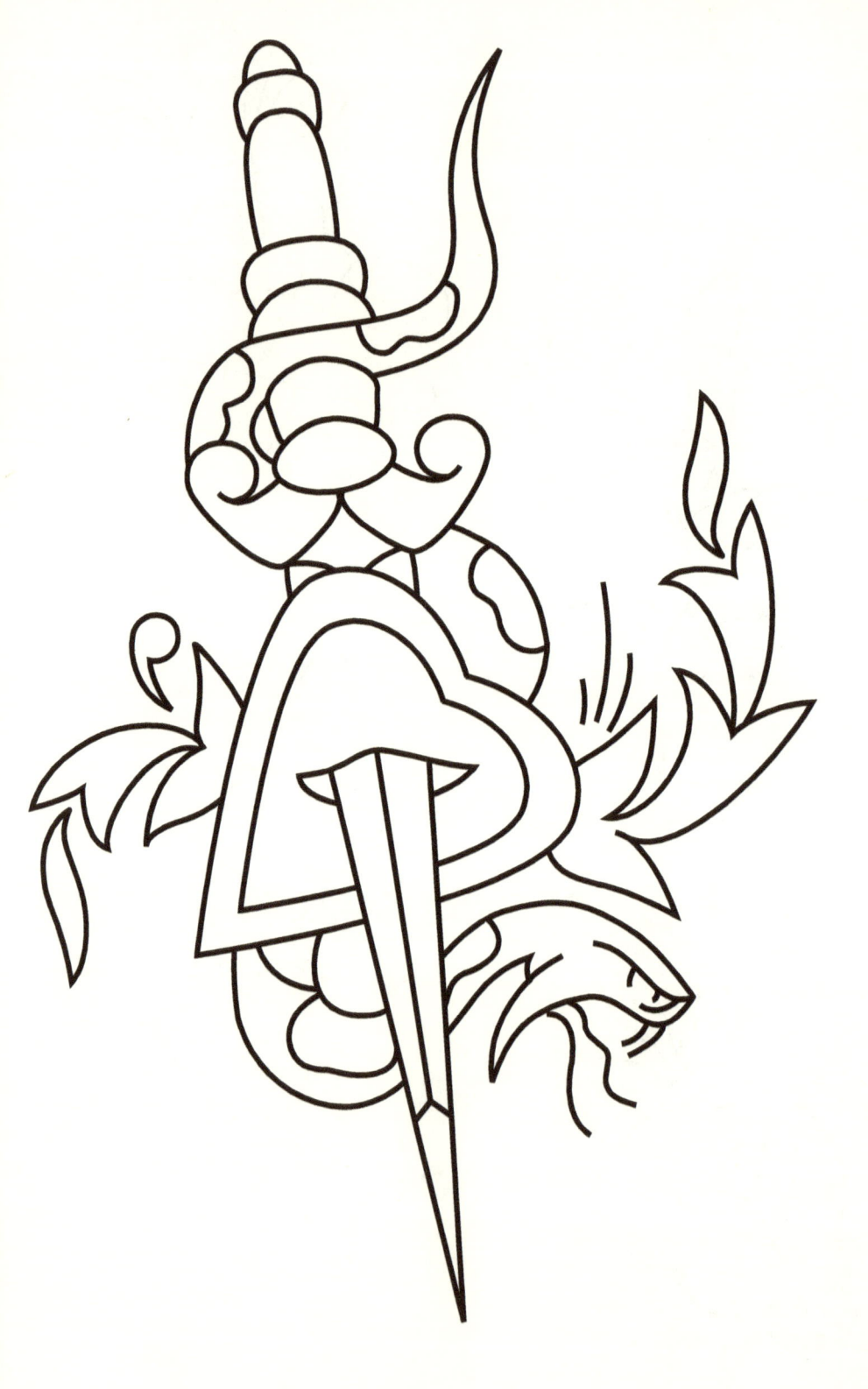

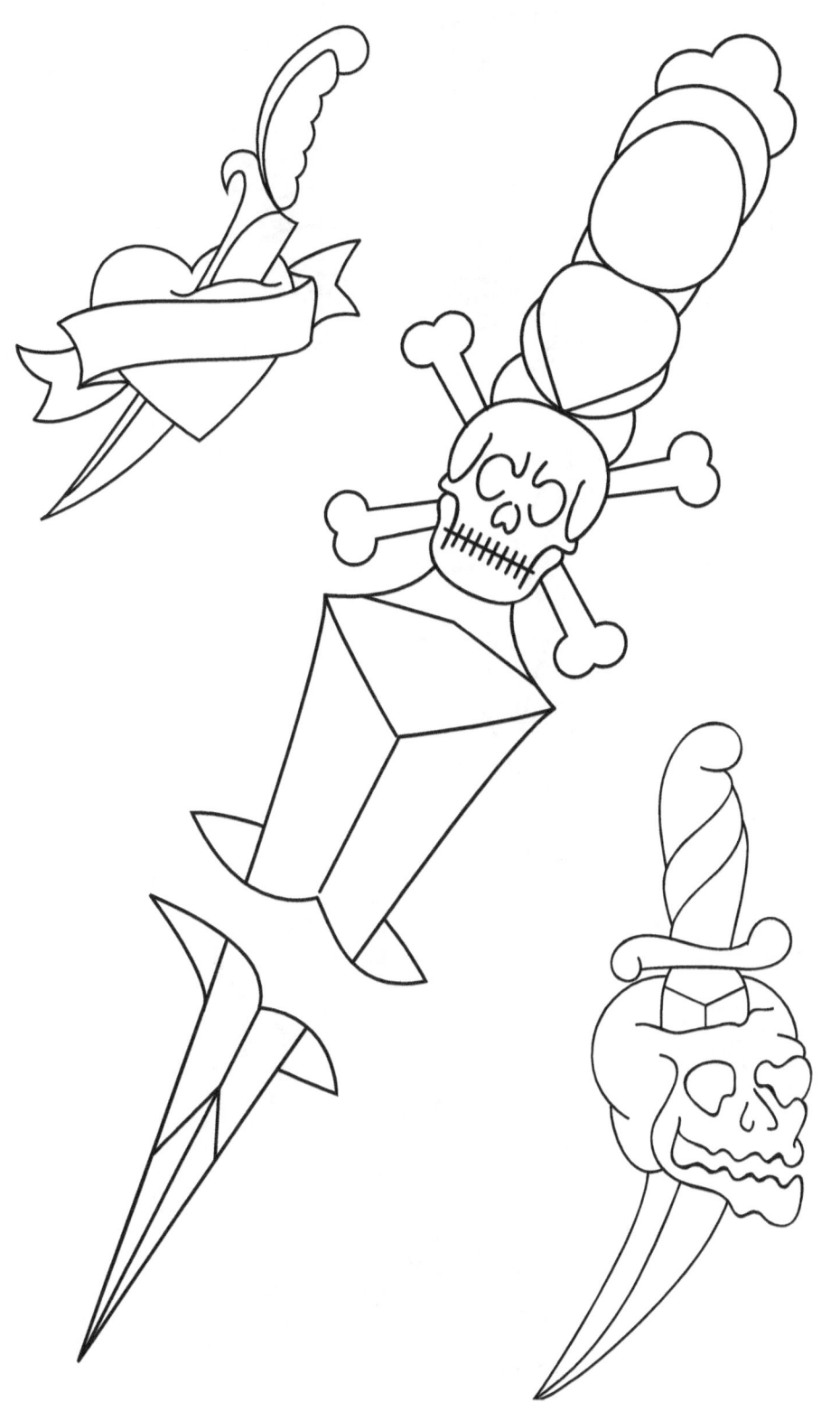

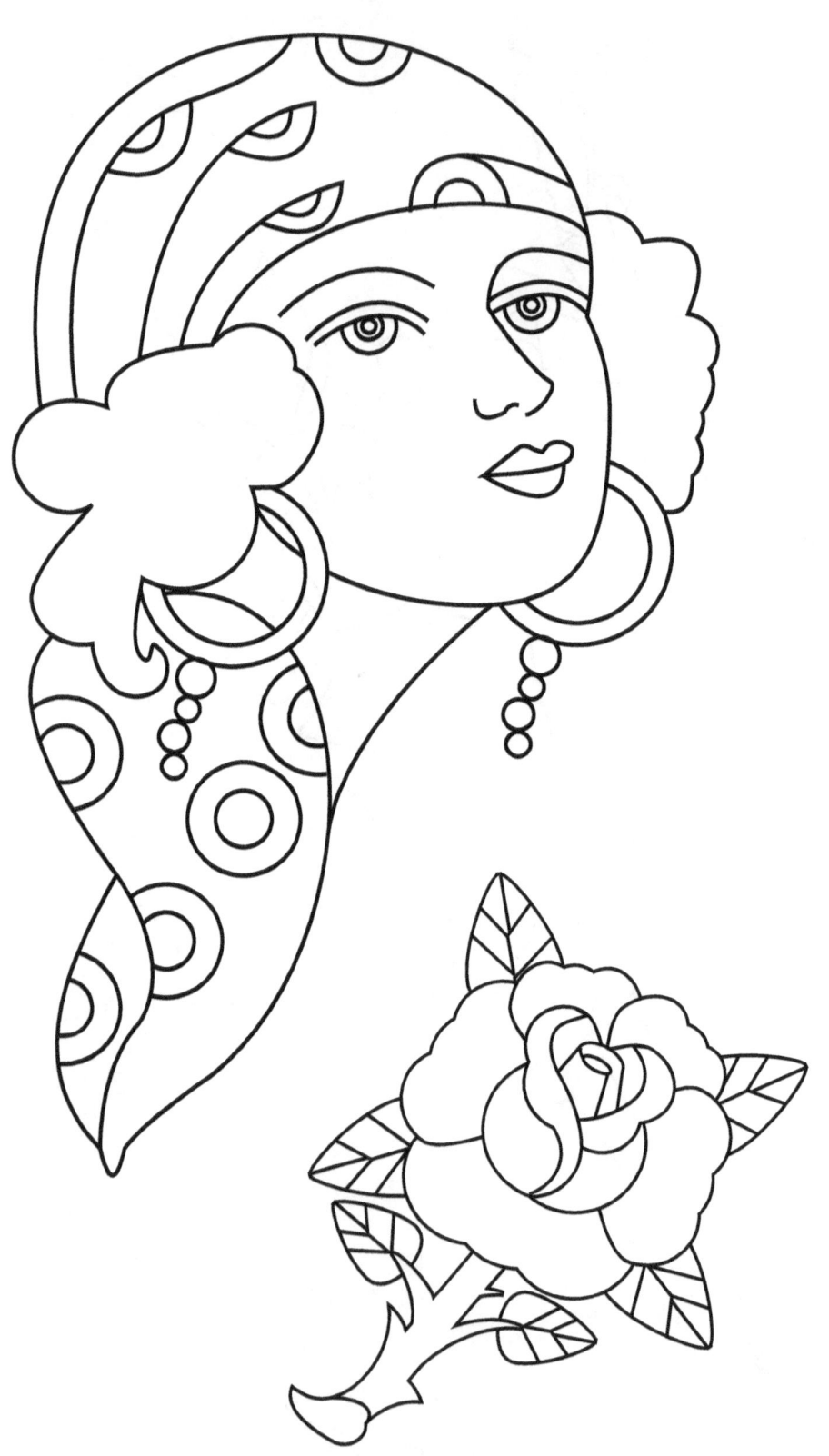

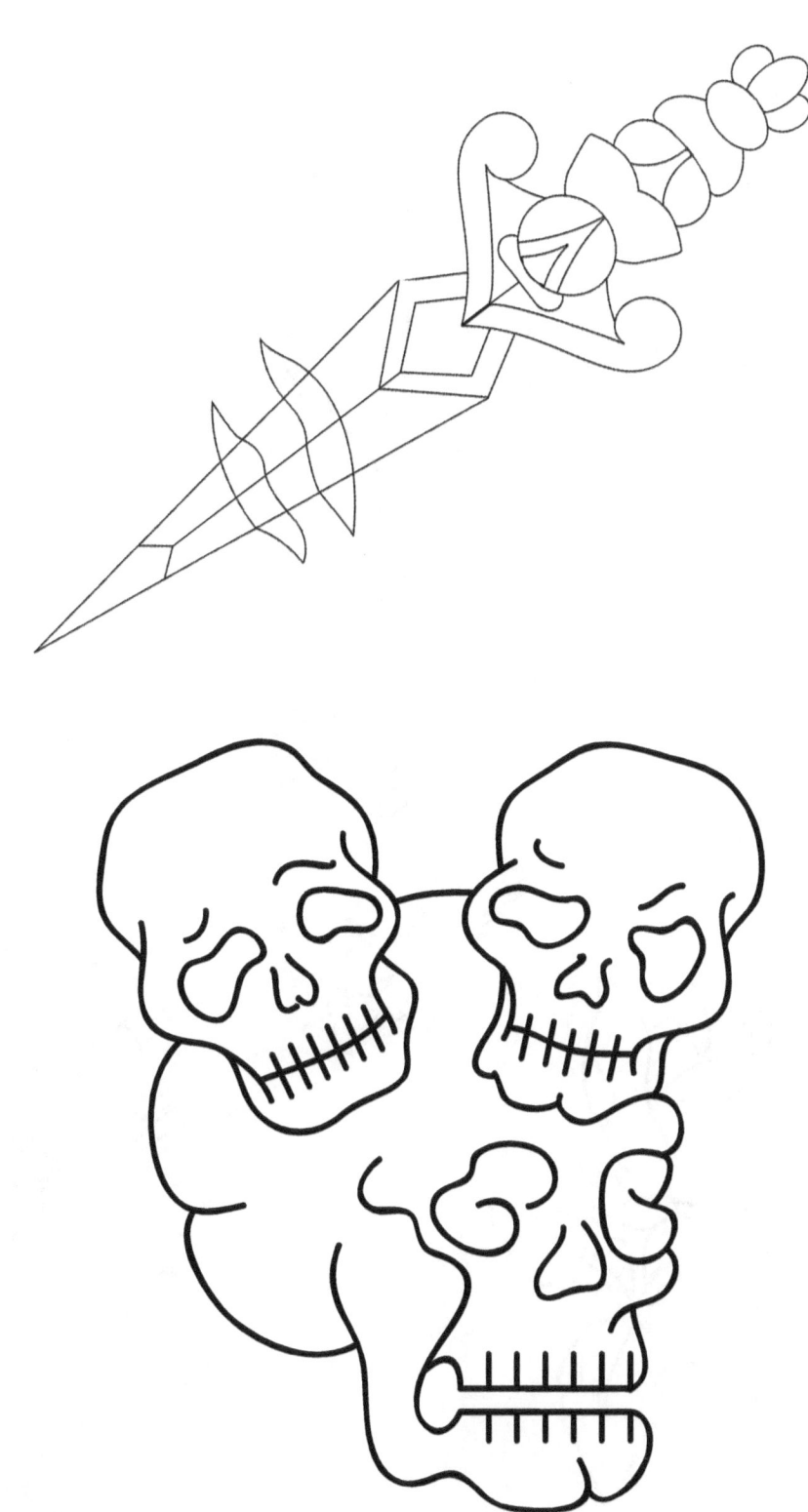

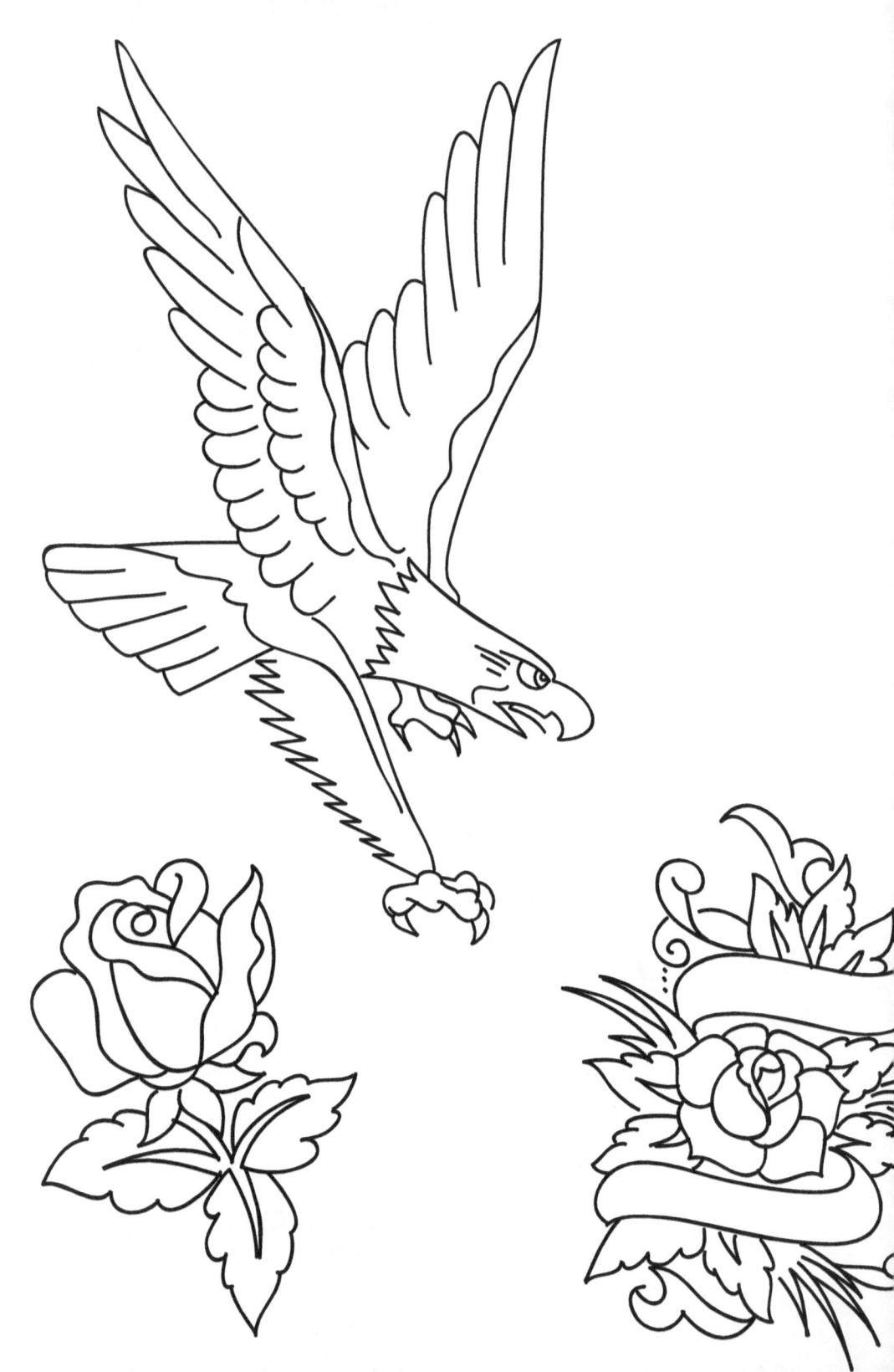

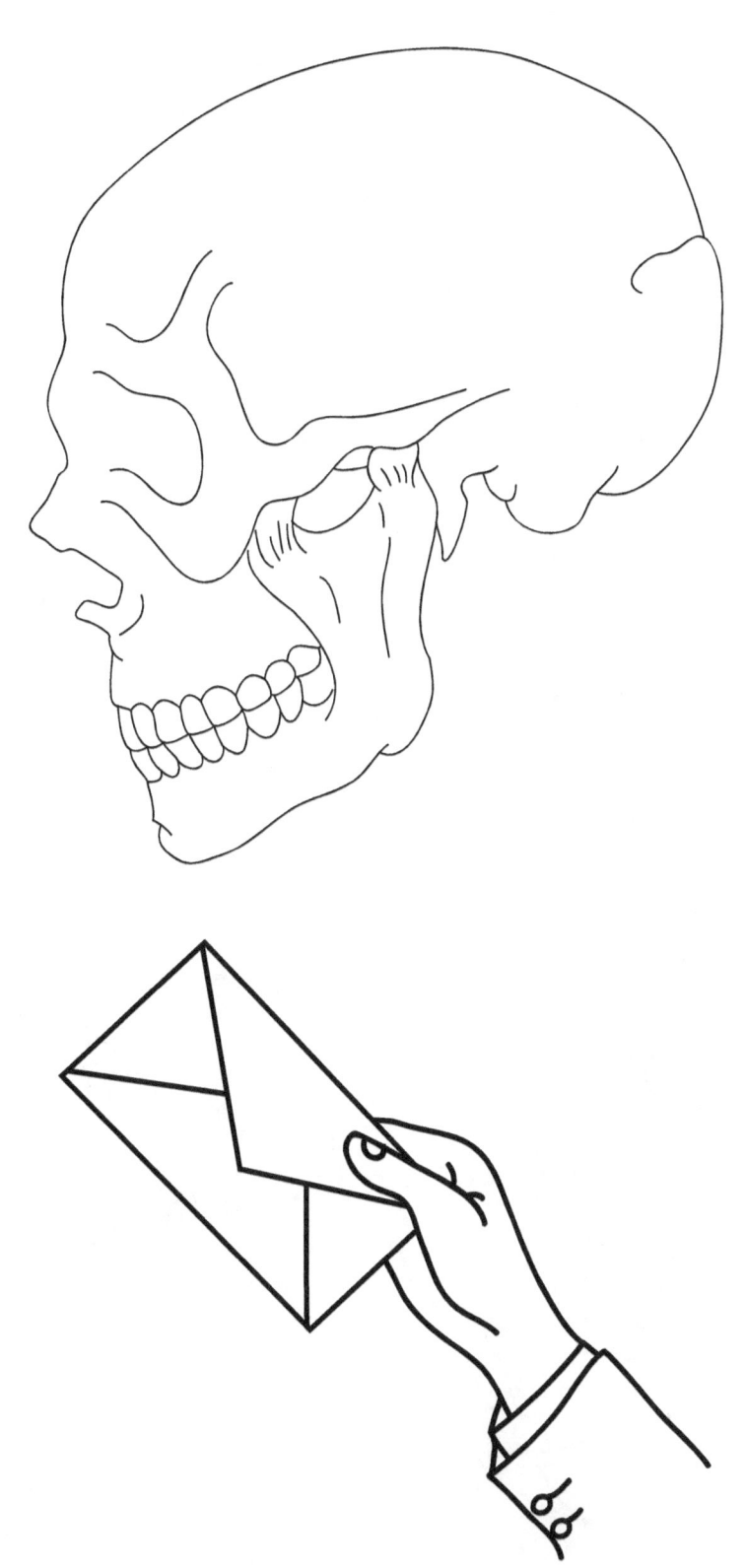

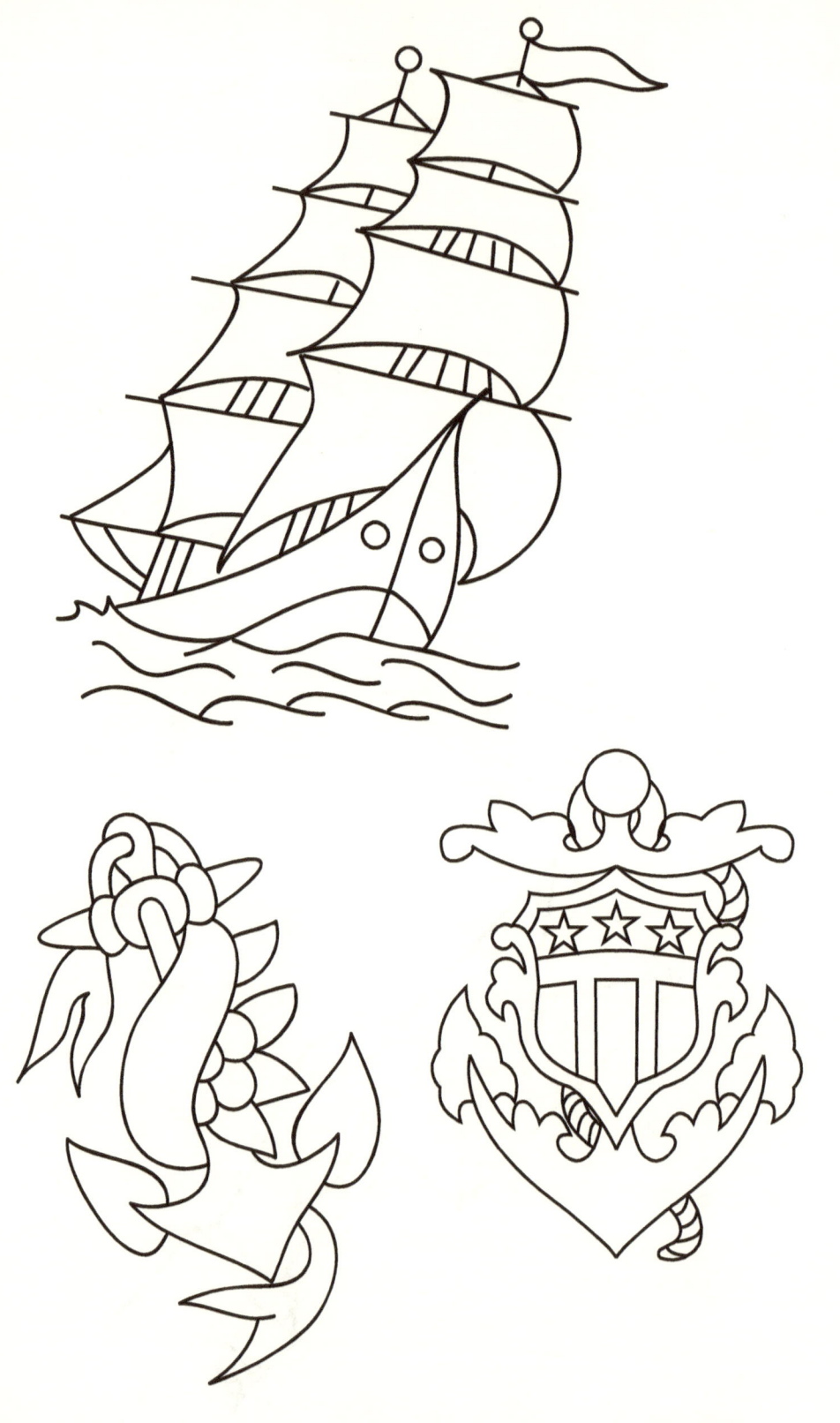

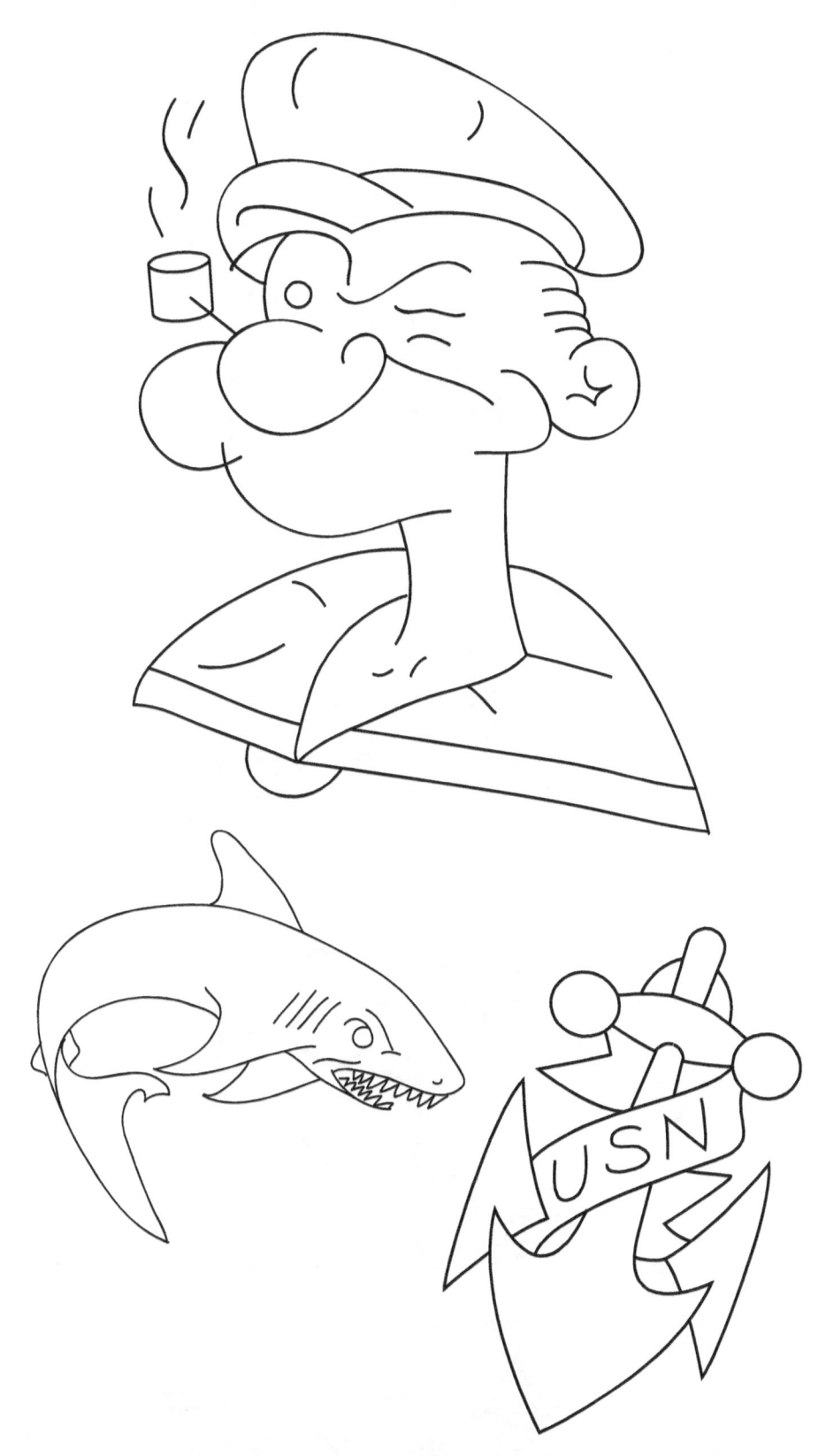

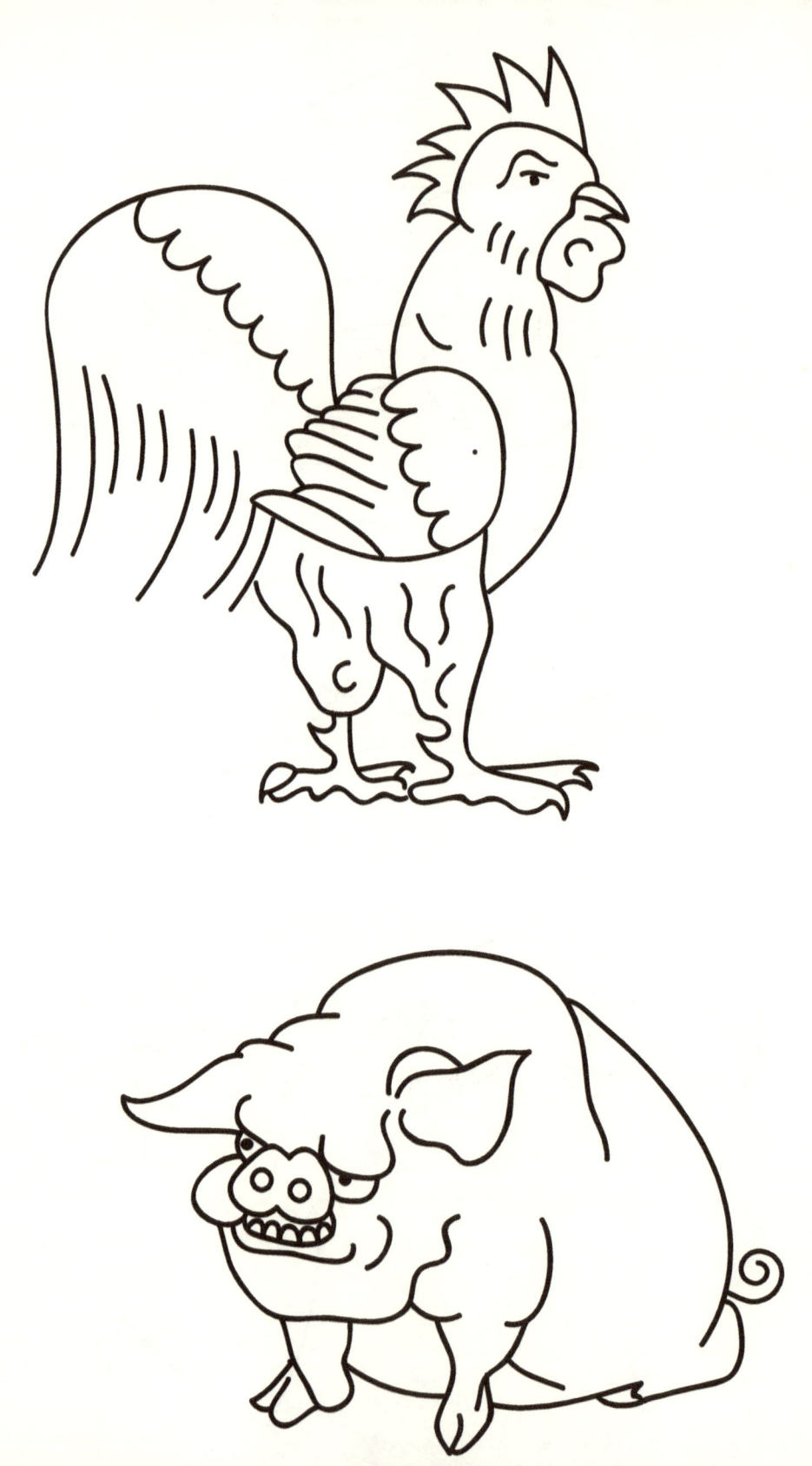

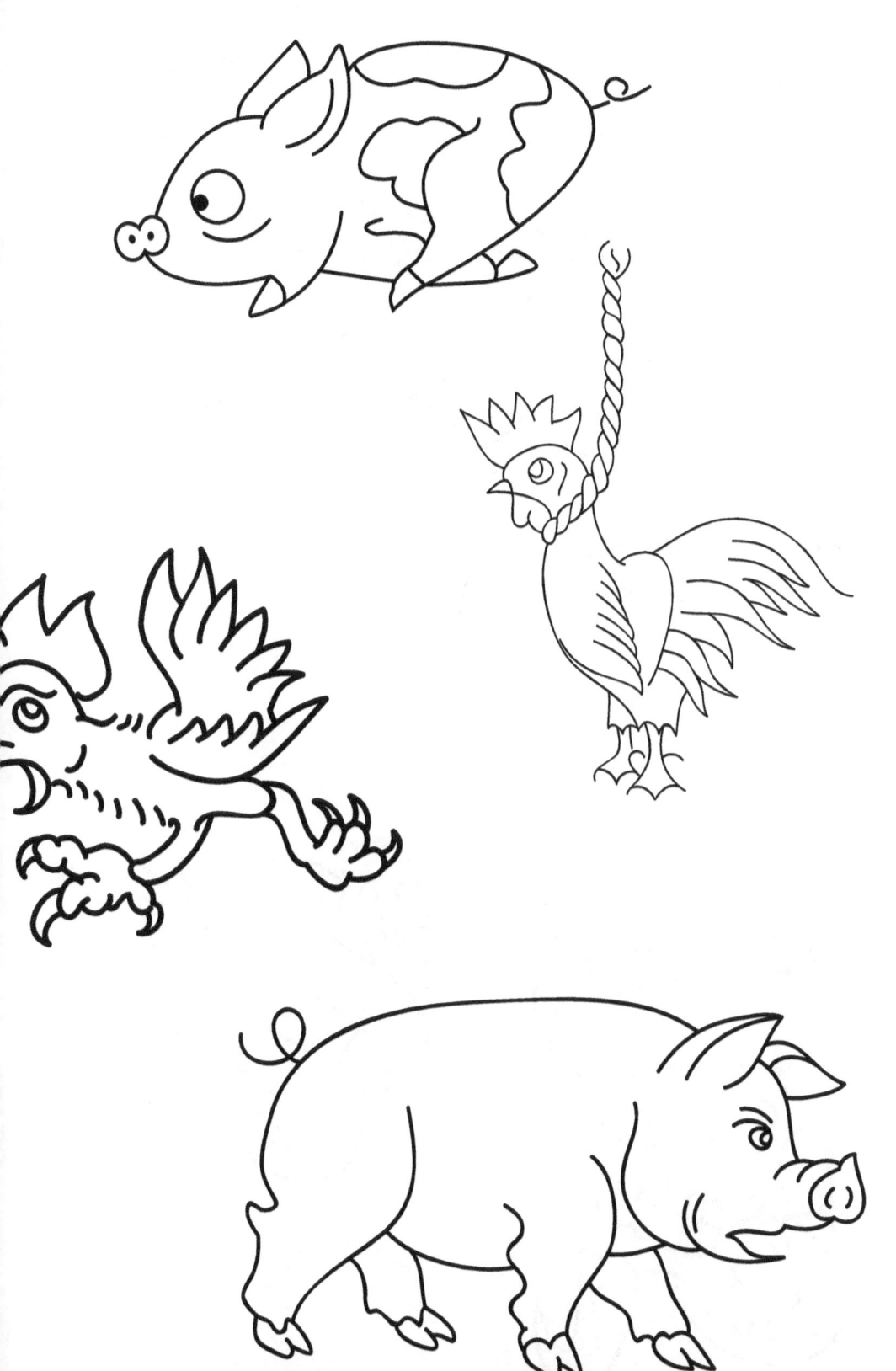

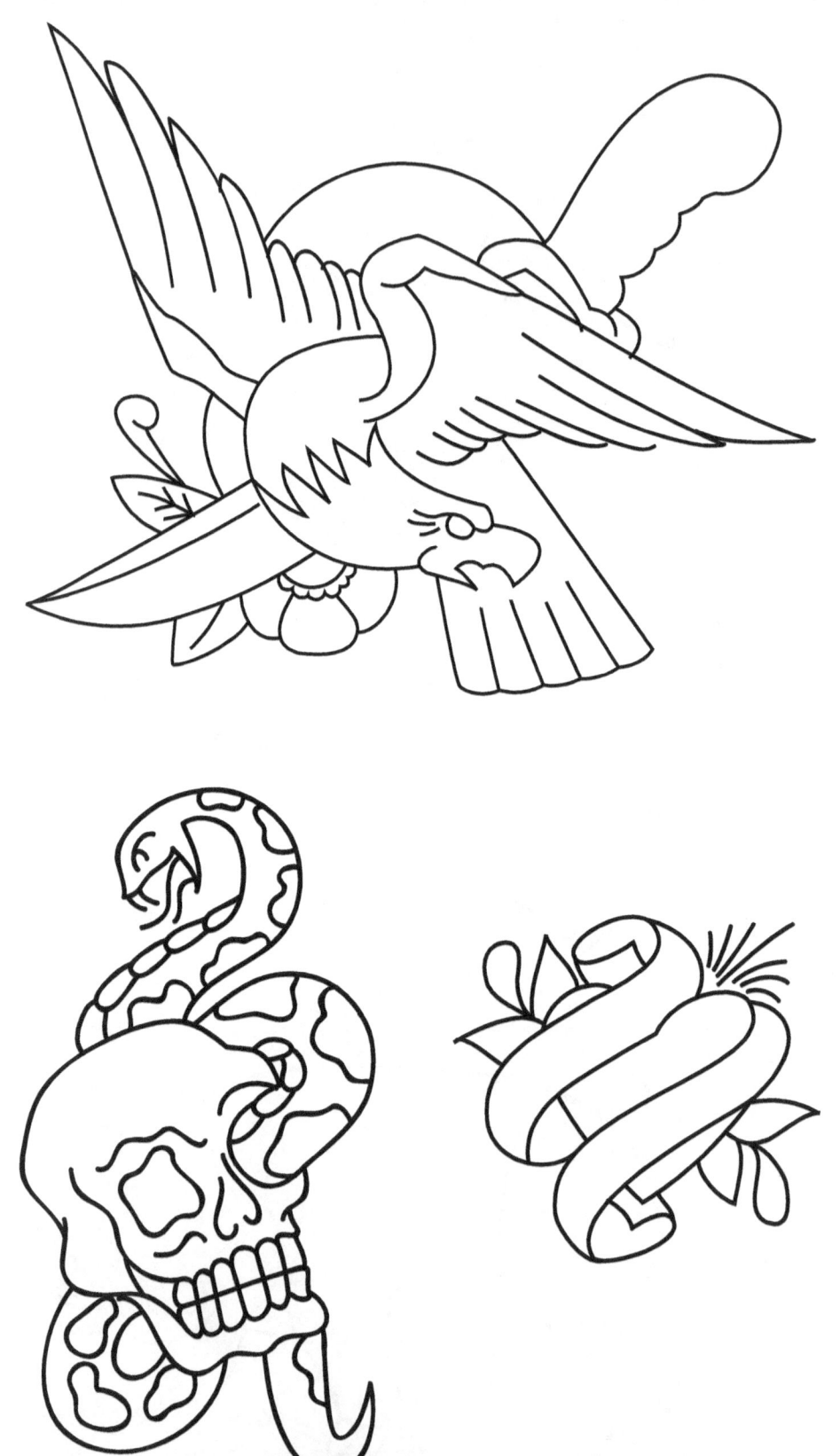

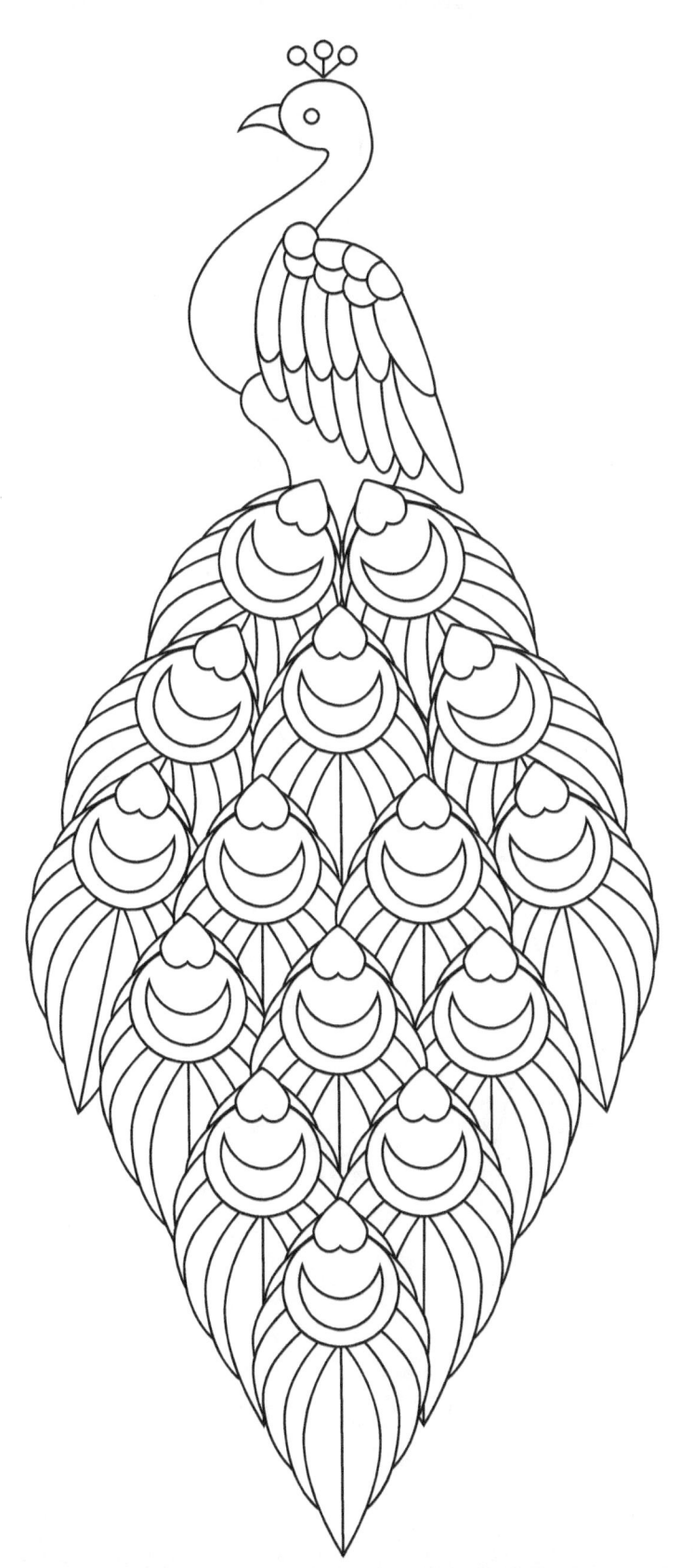

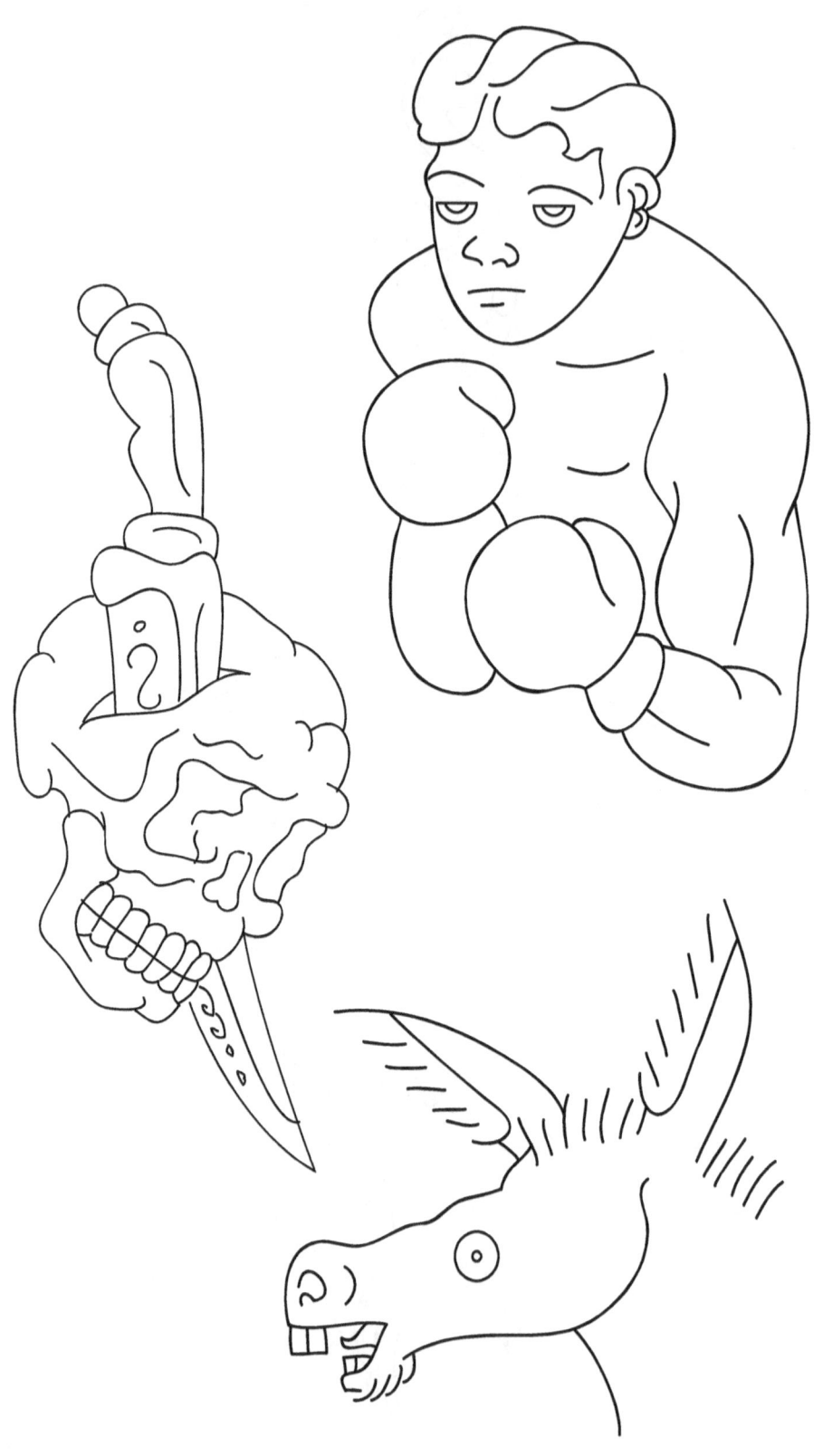

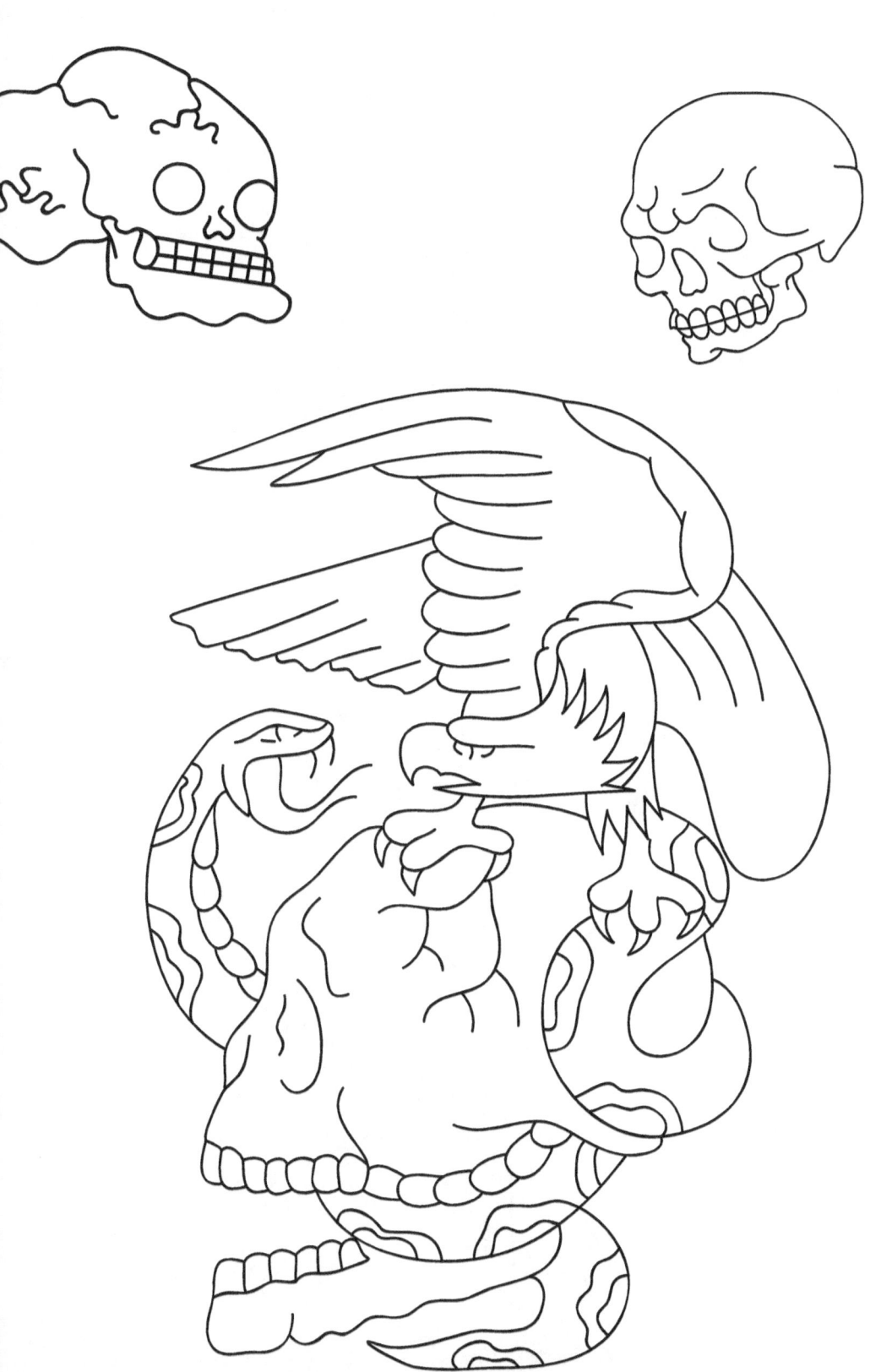

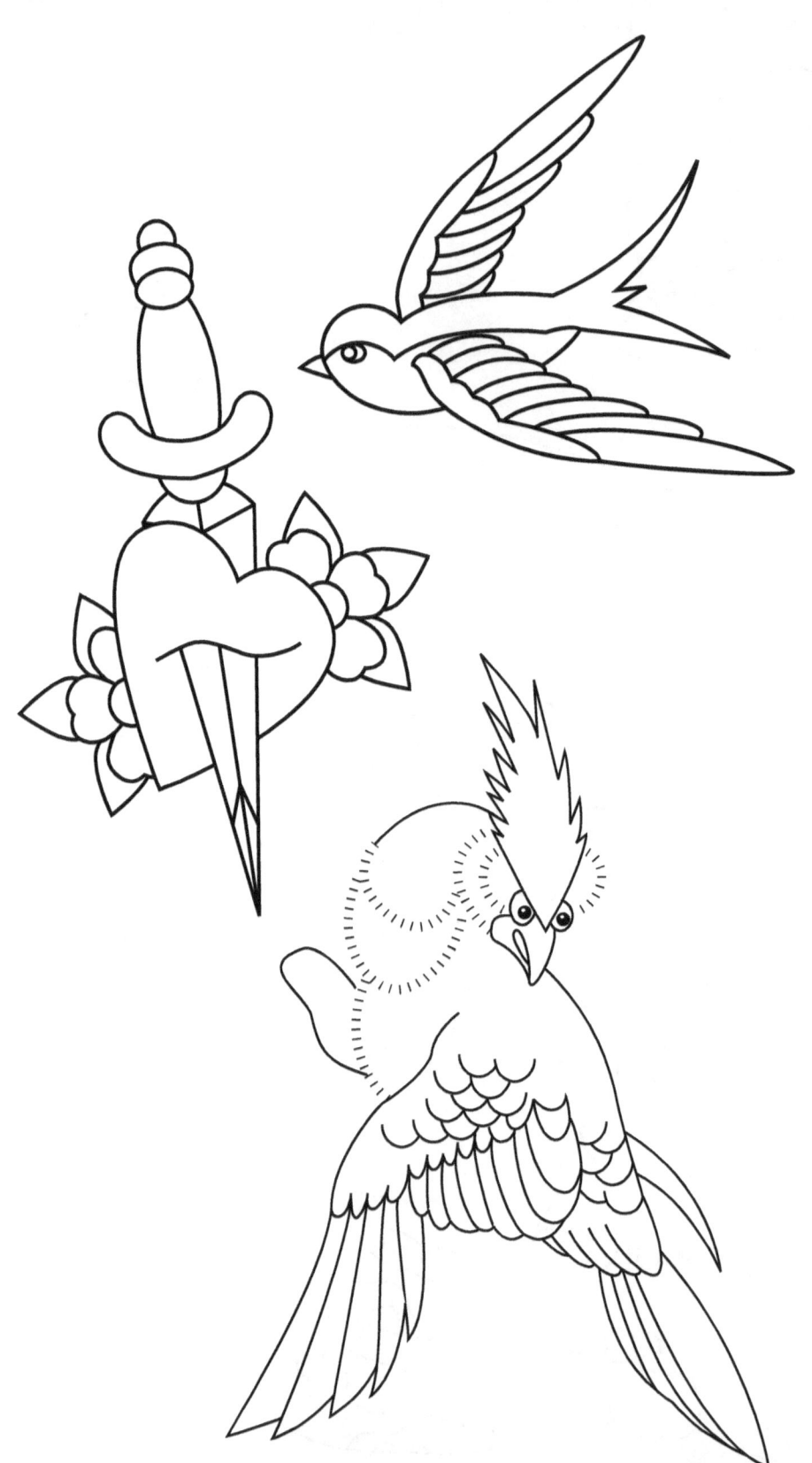

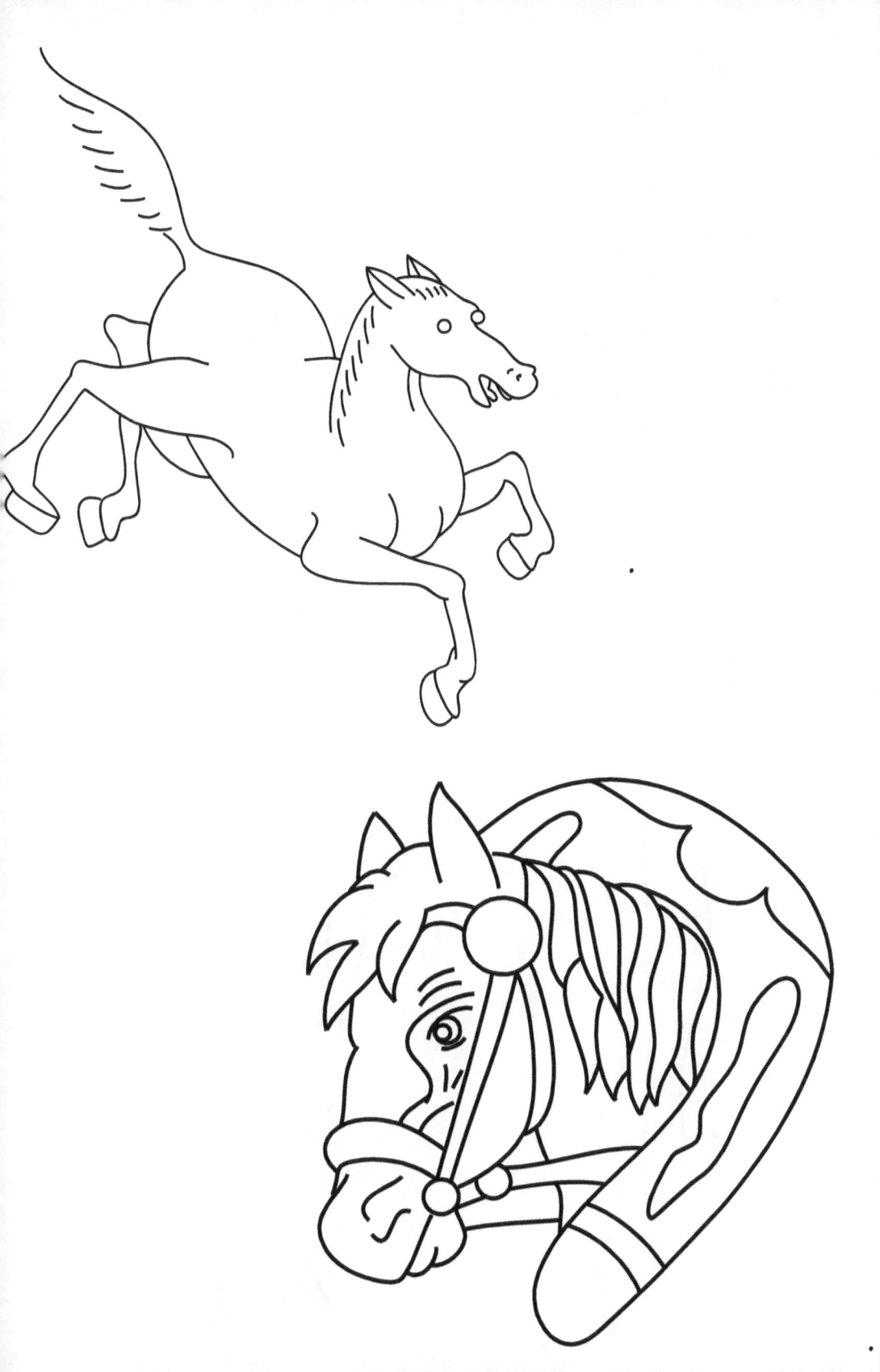

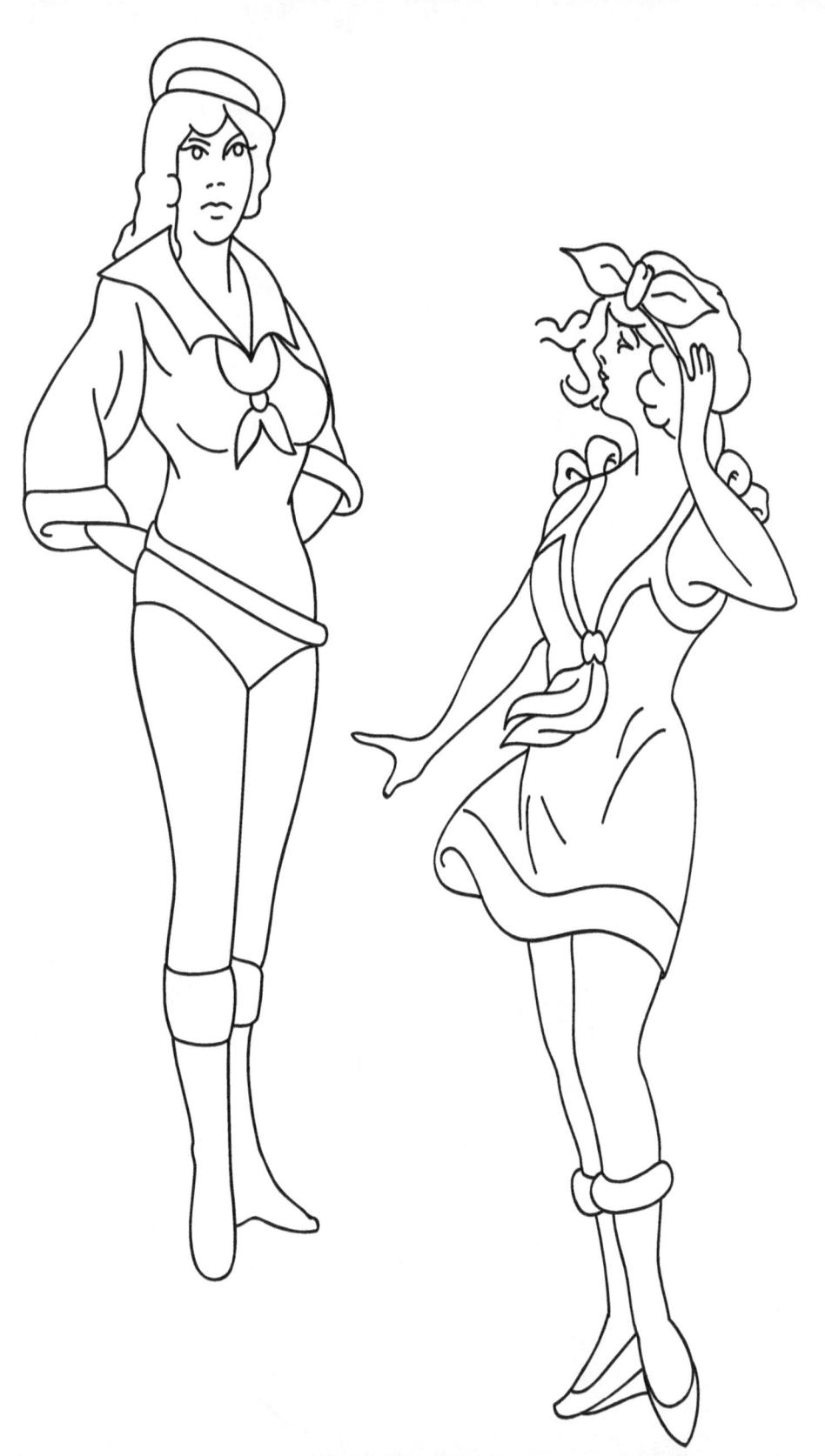

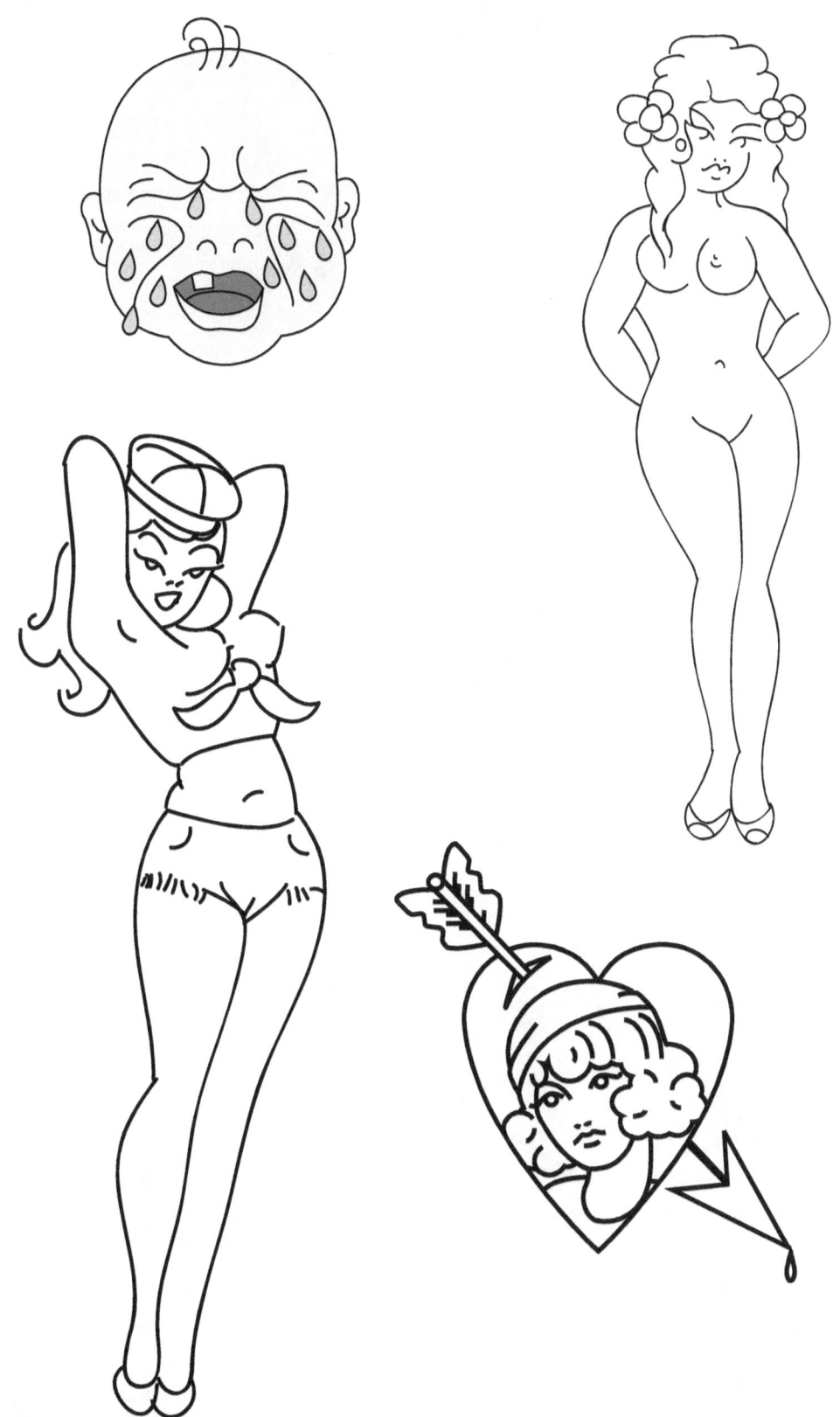

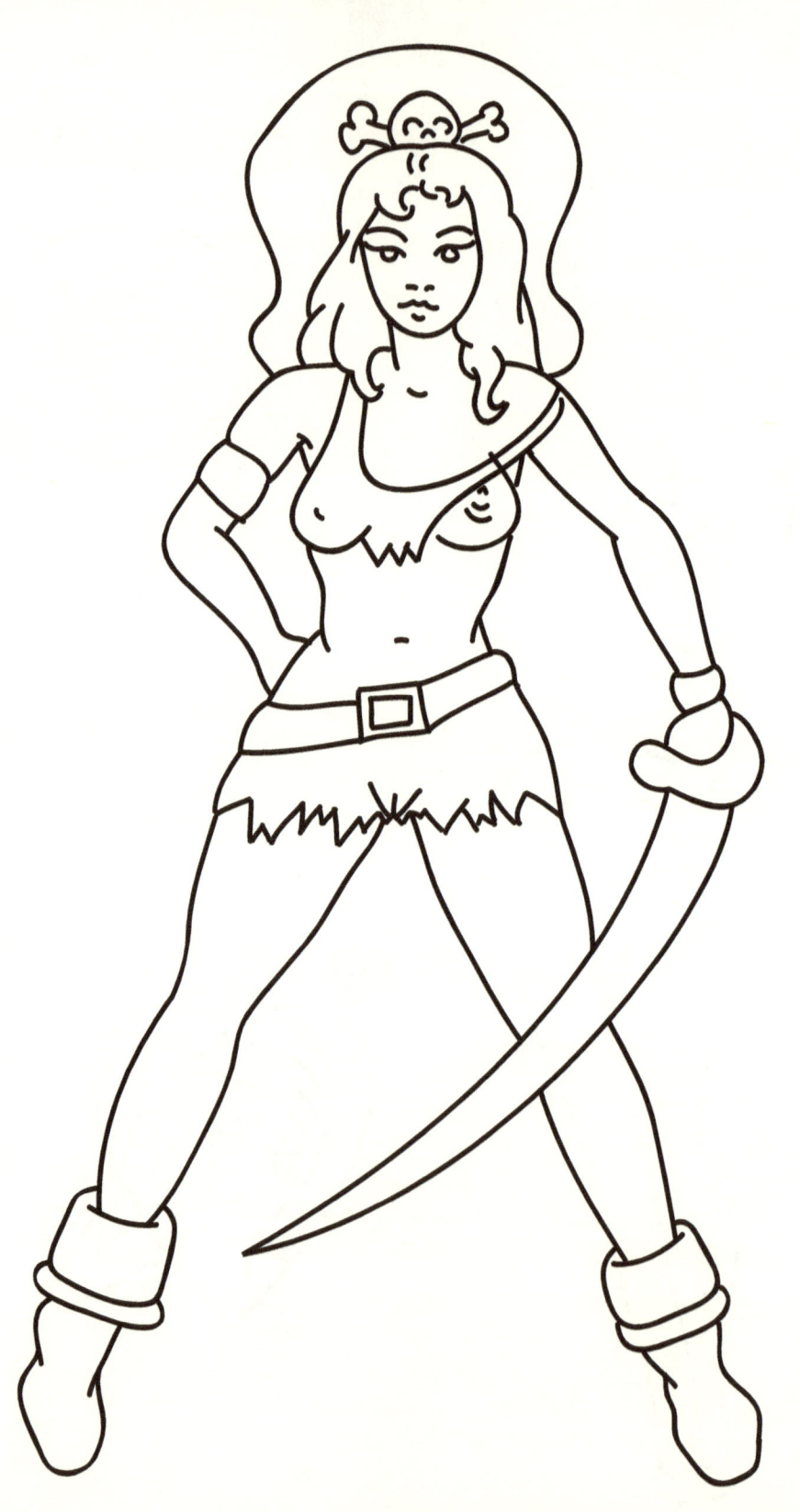

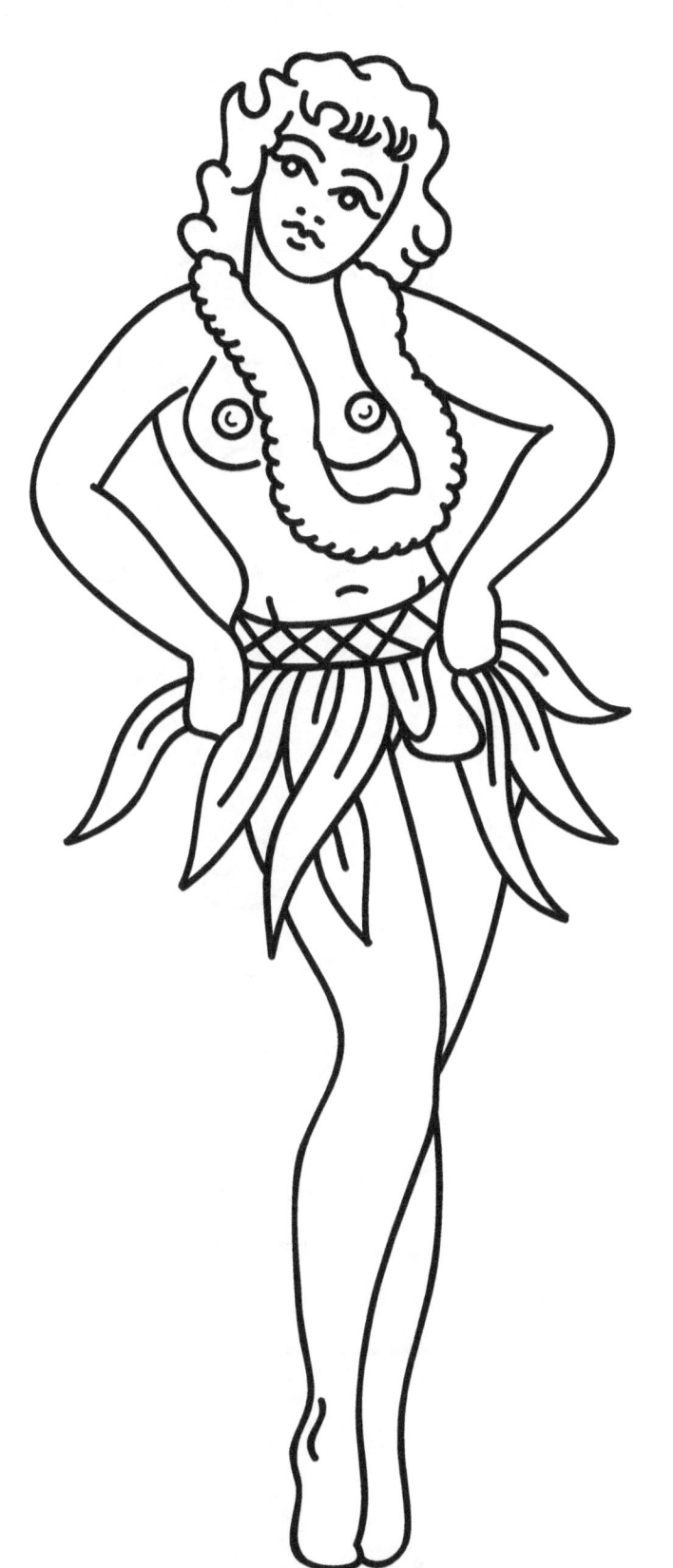

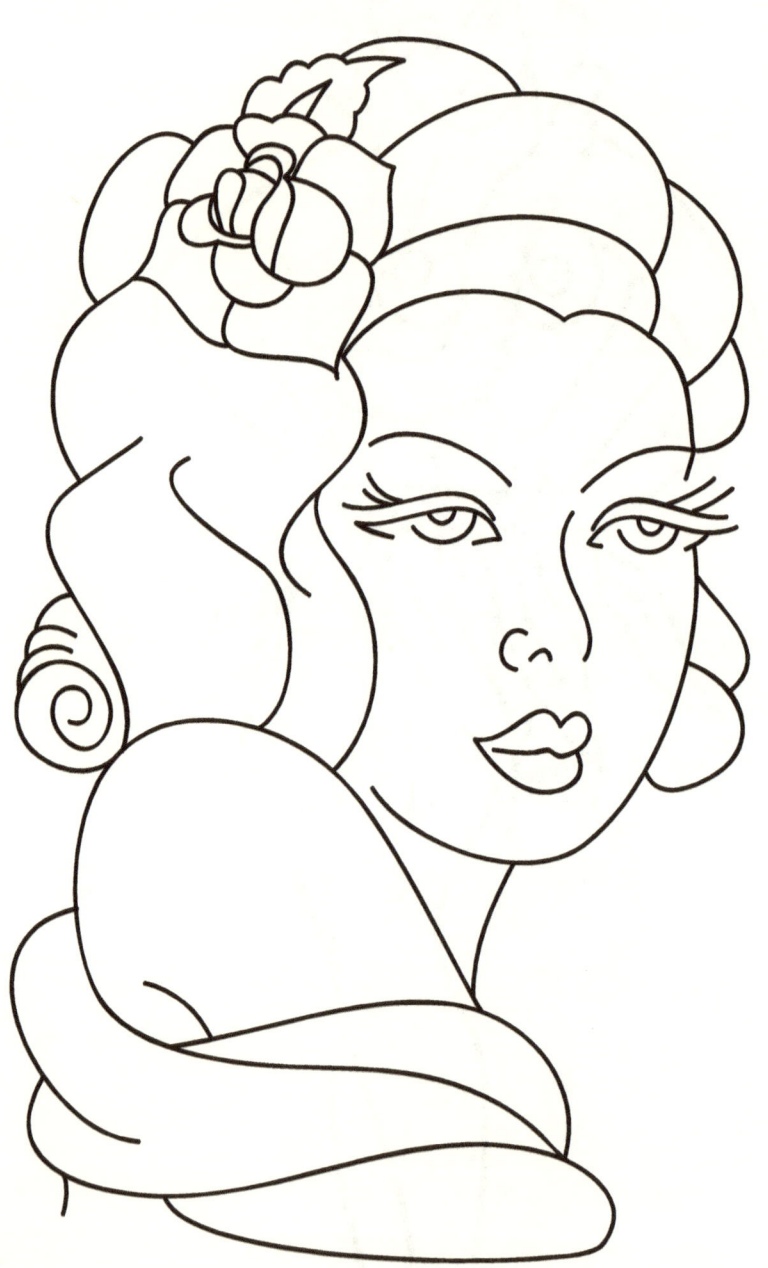

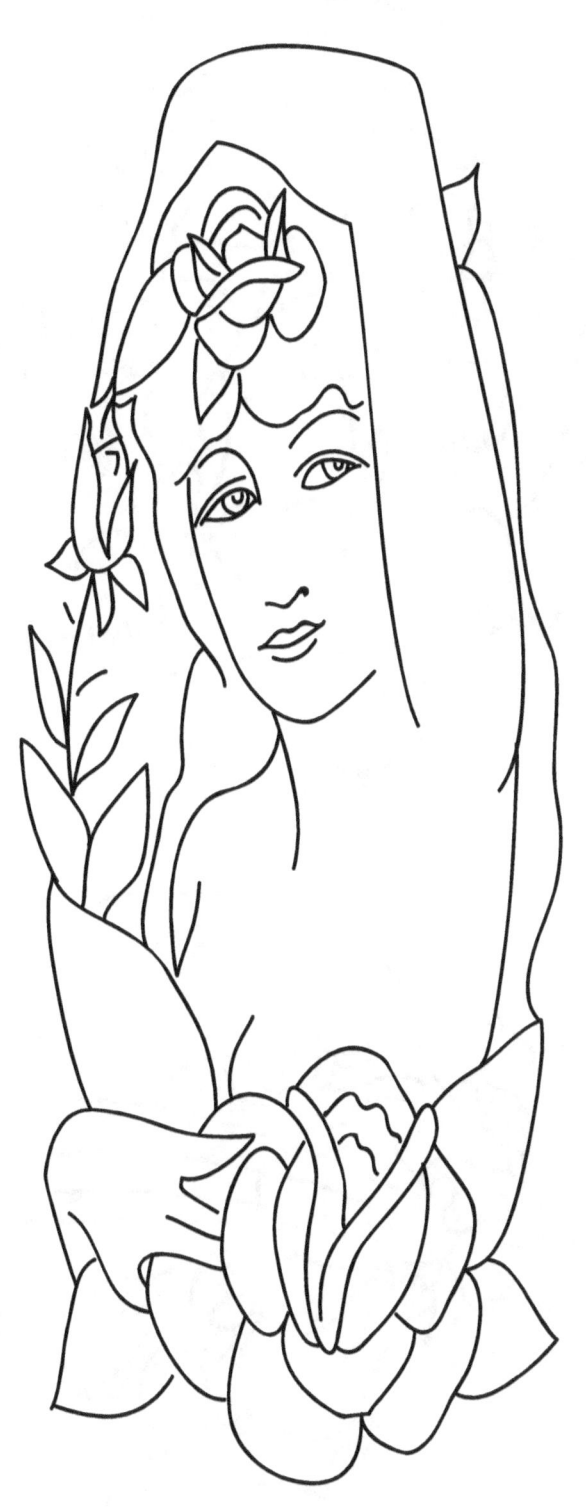

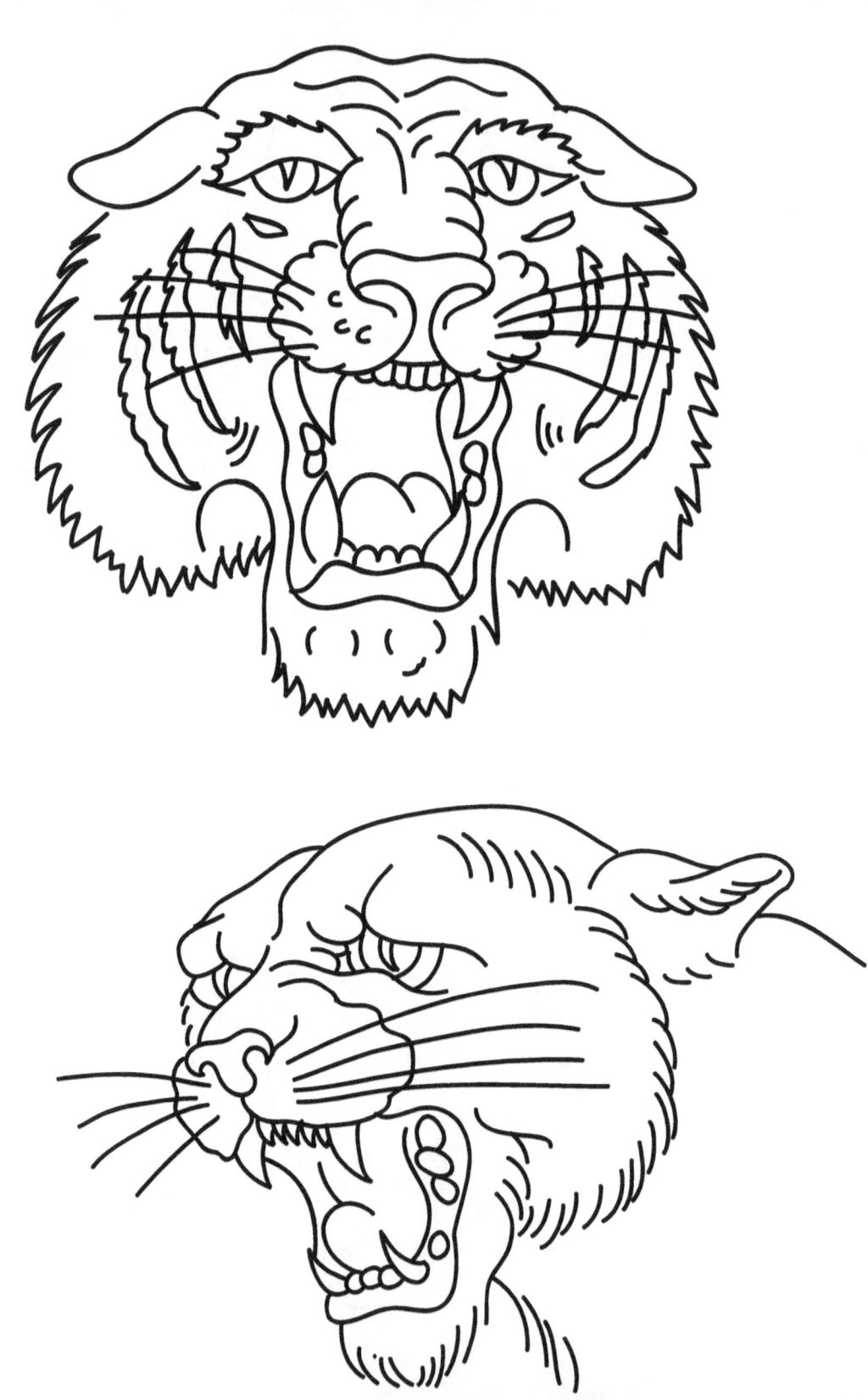

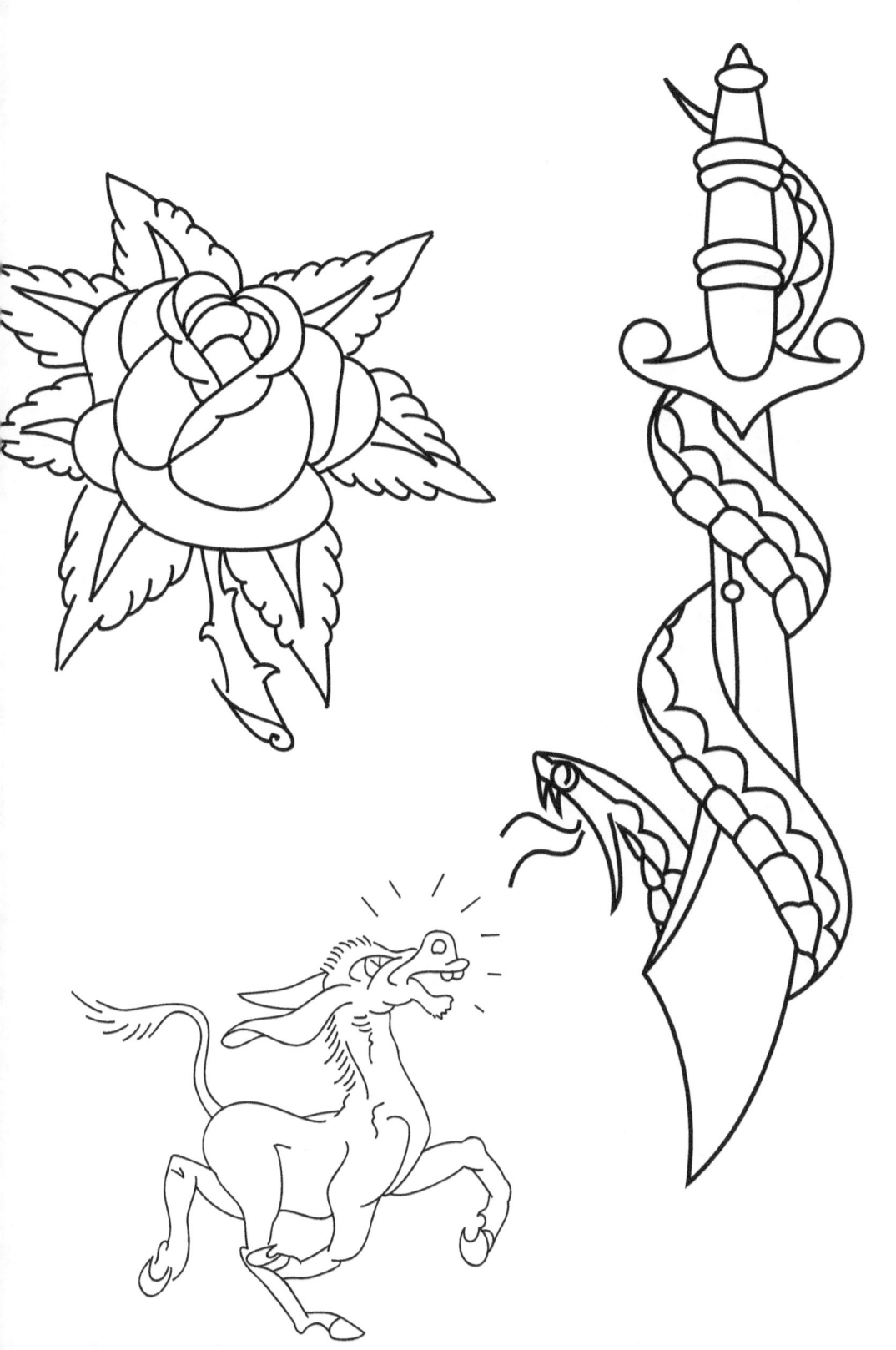

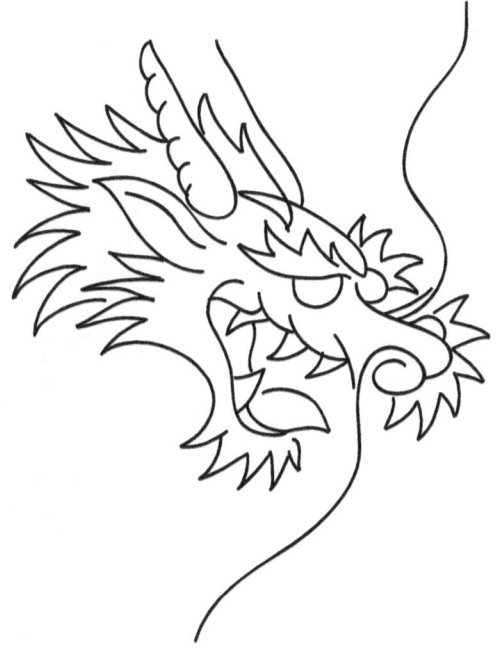

"Japanese"

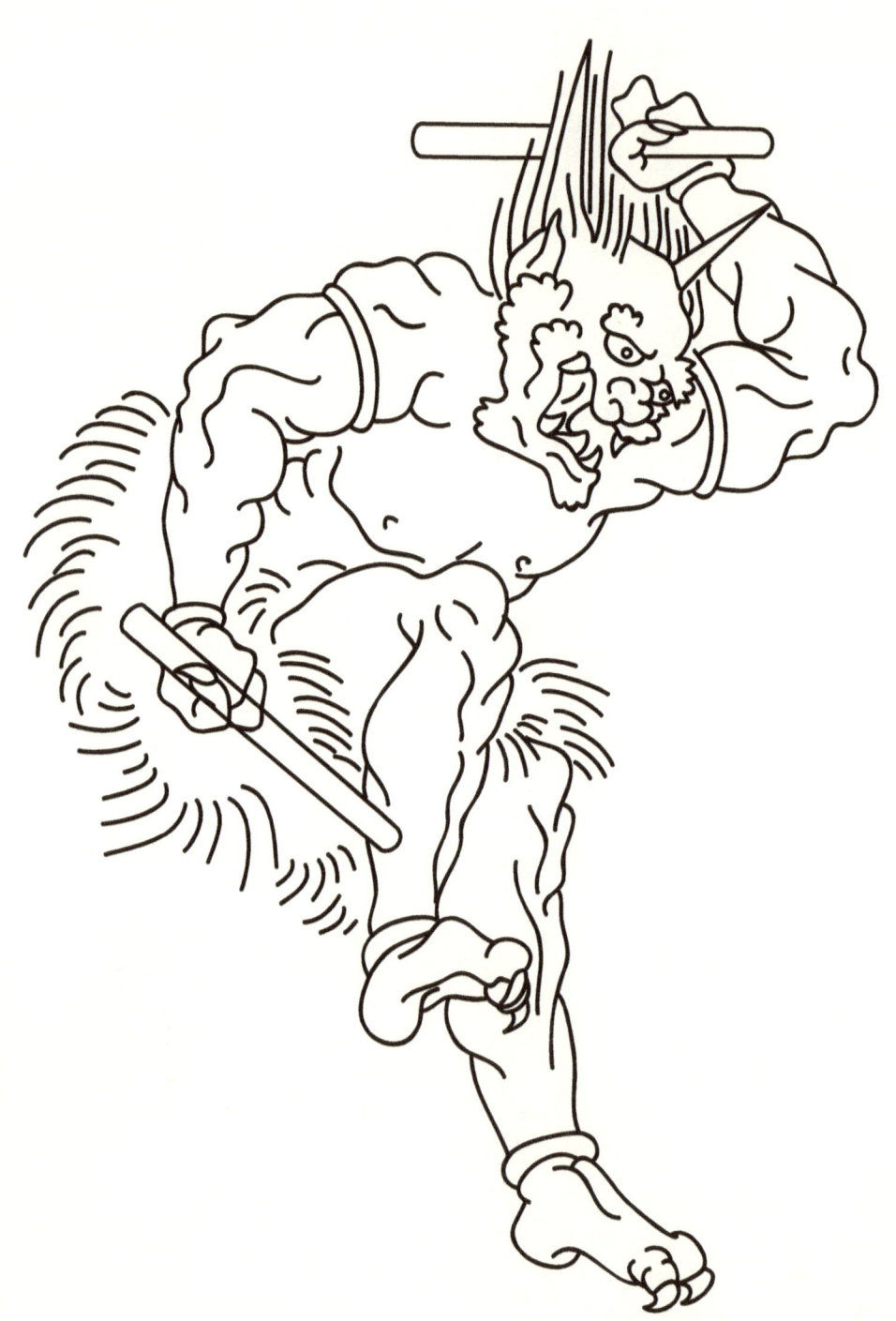

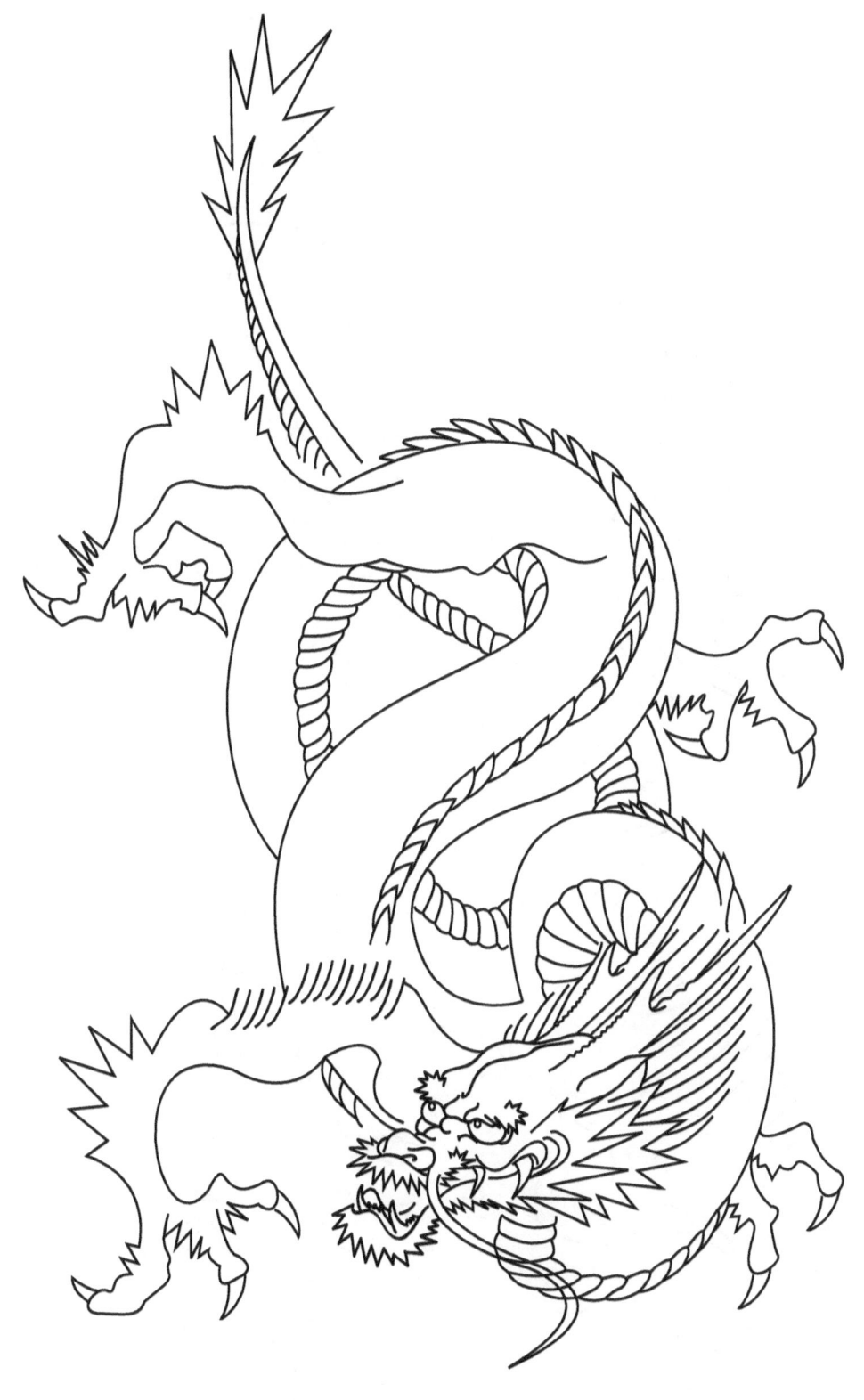

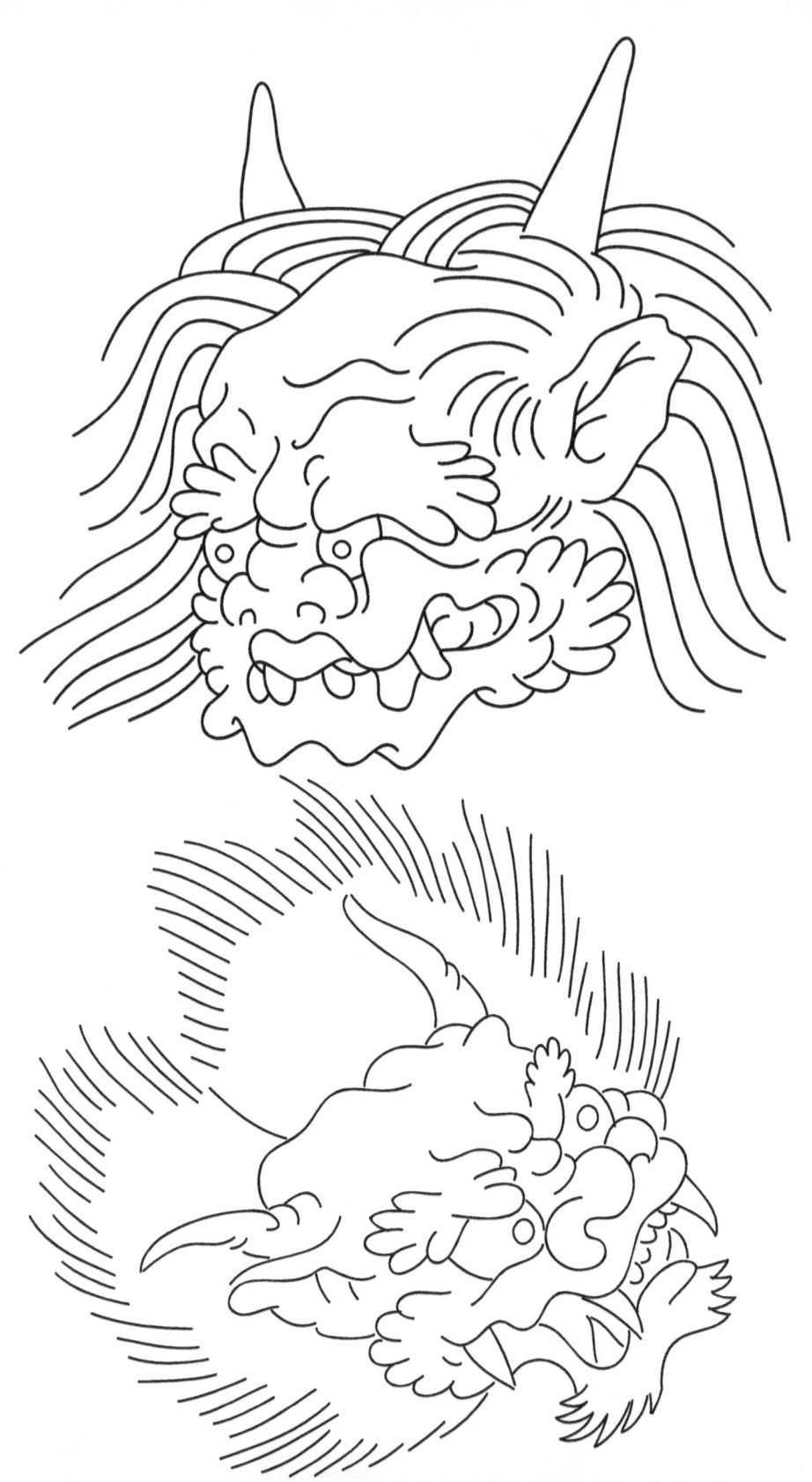

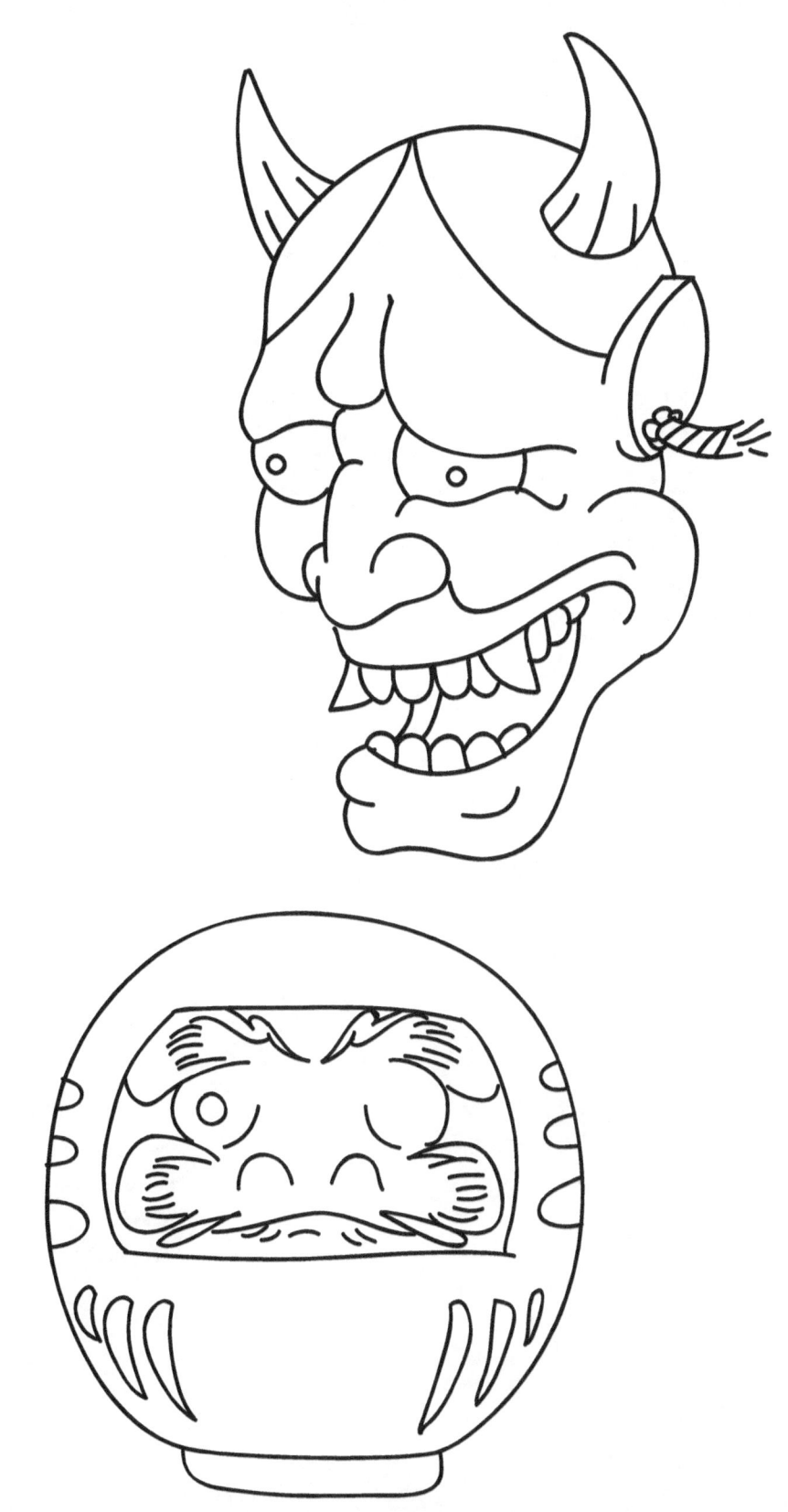

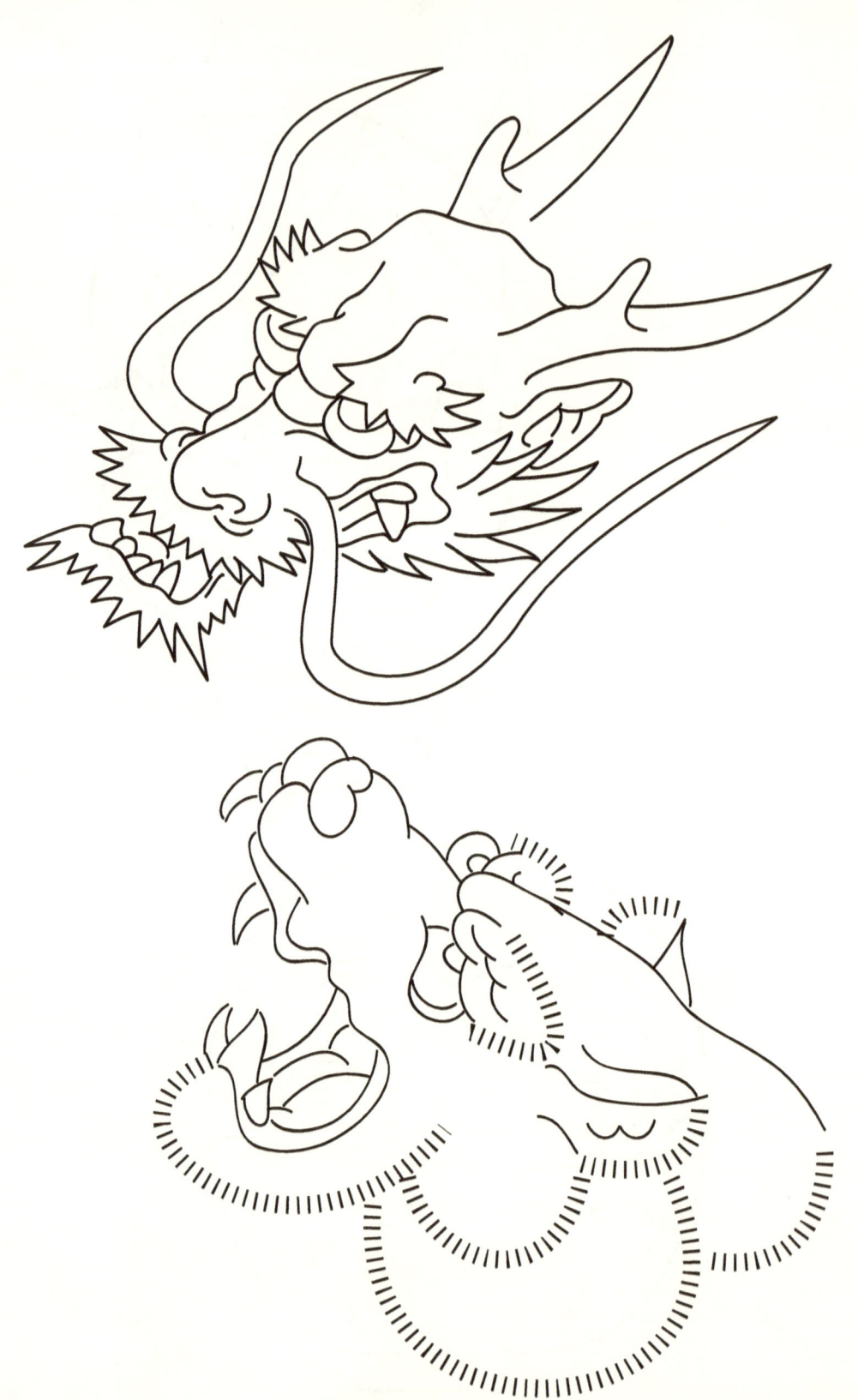

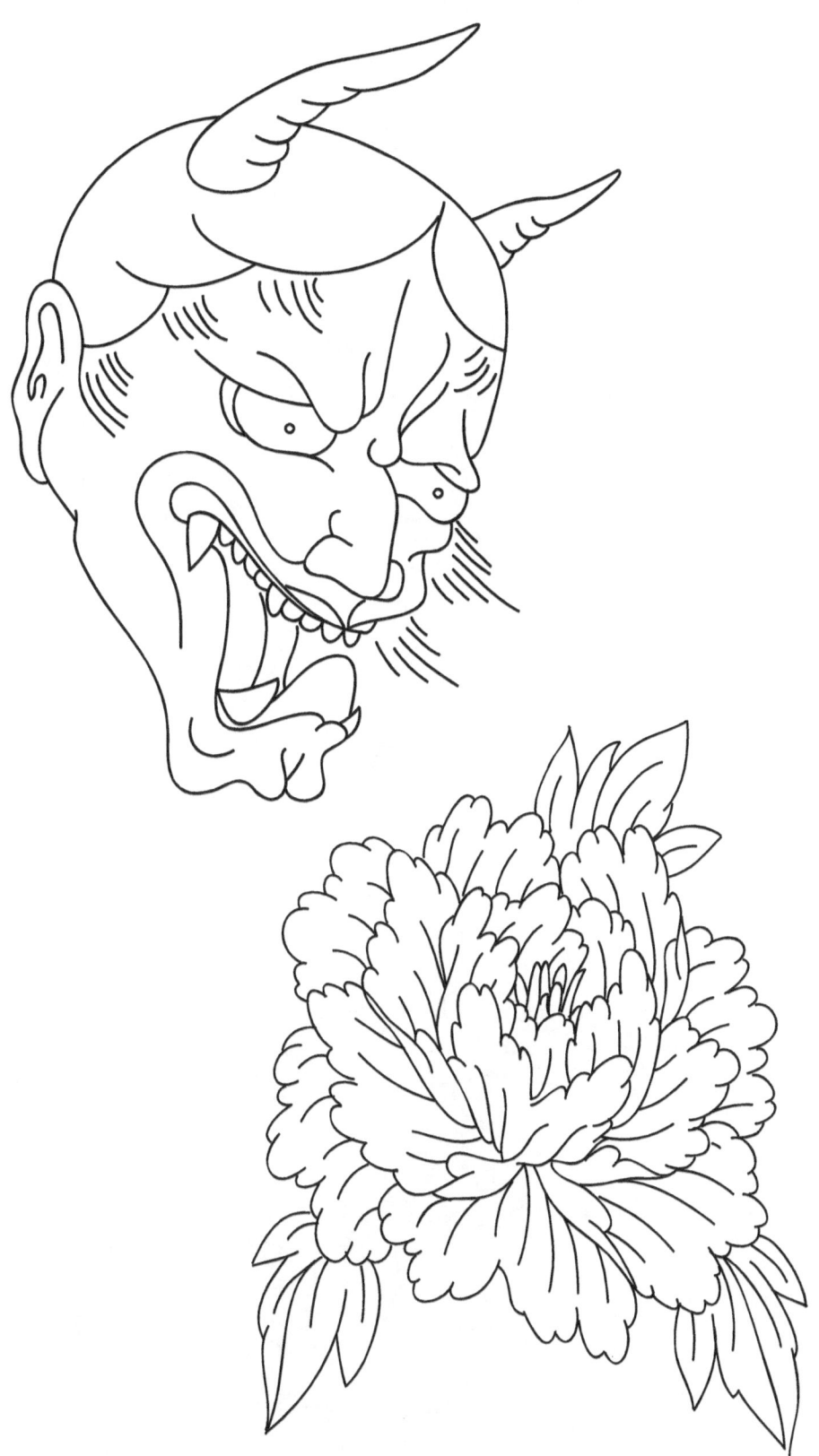

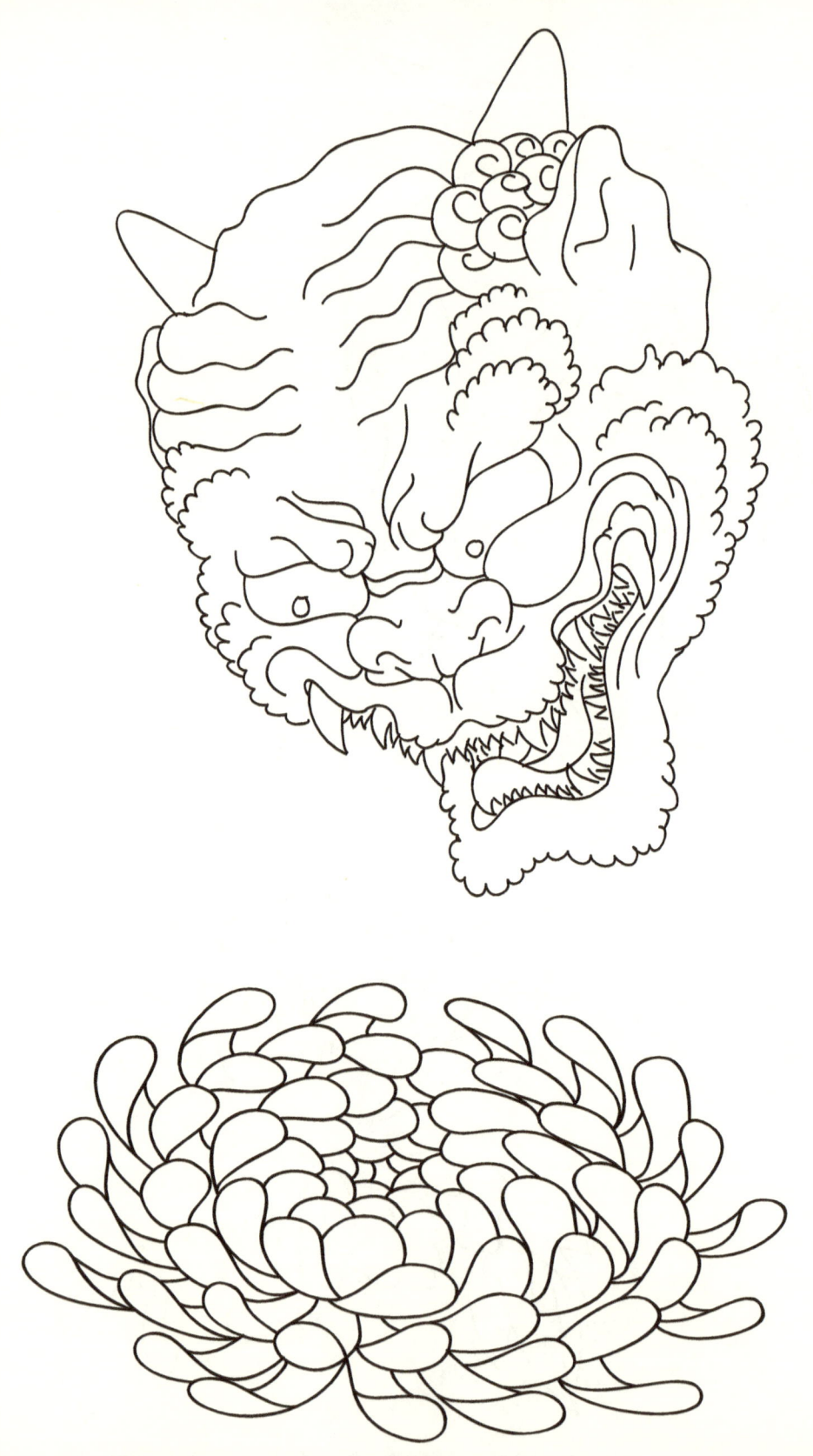

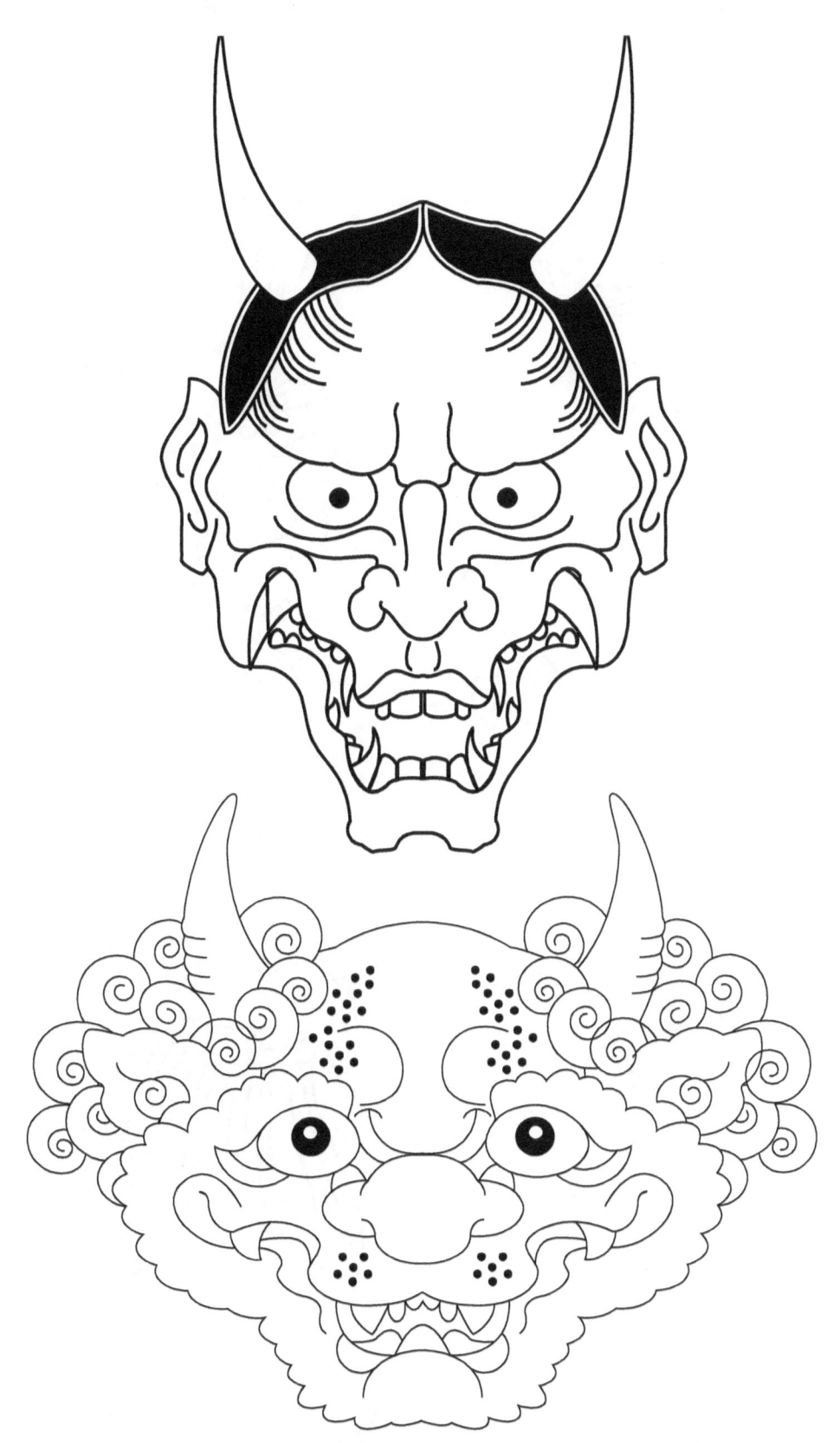

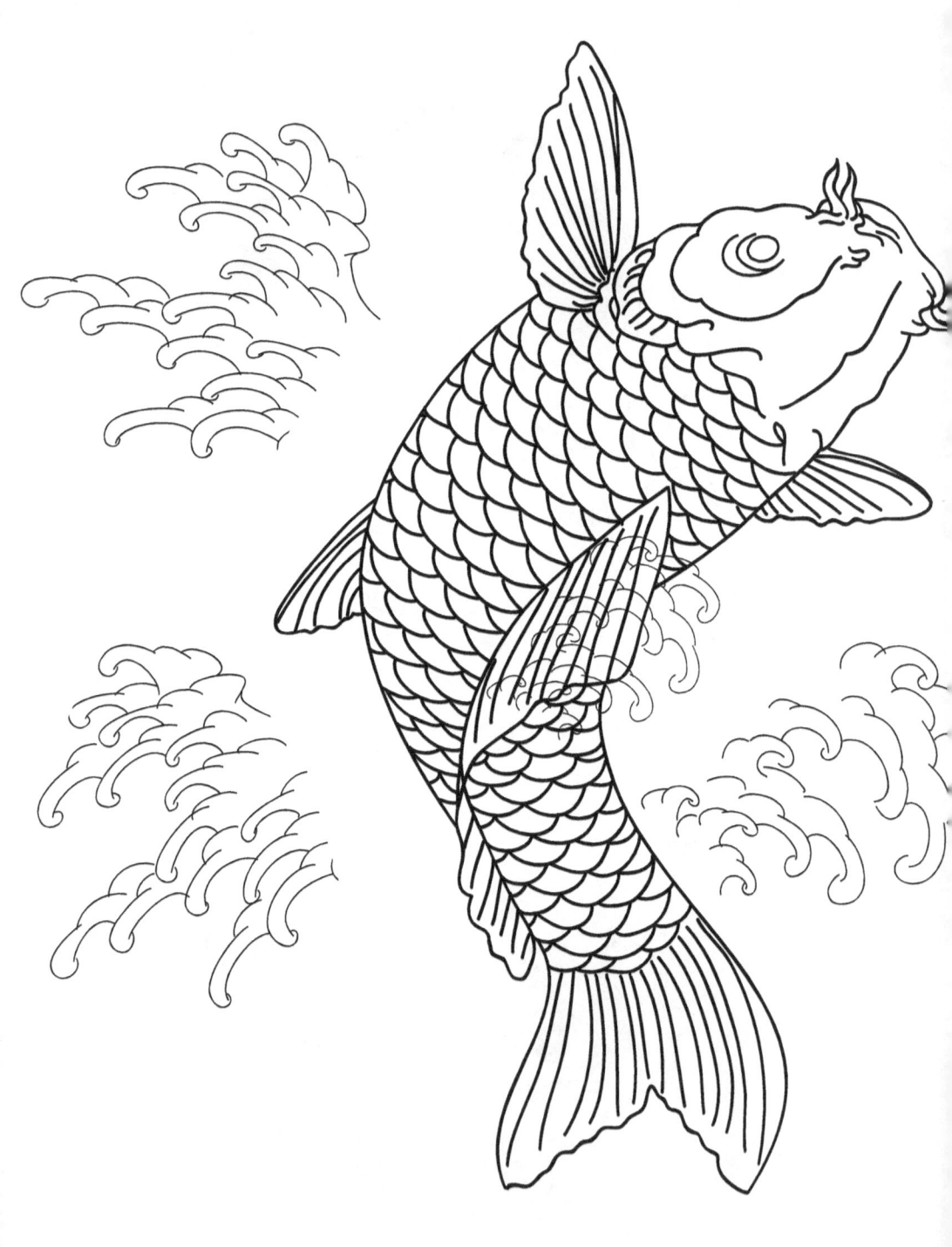

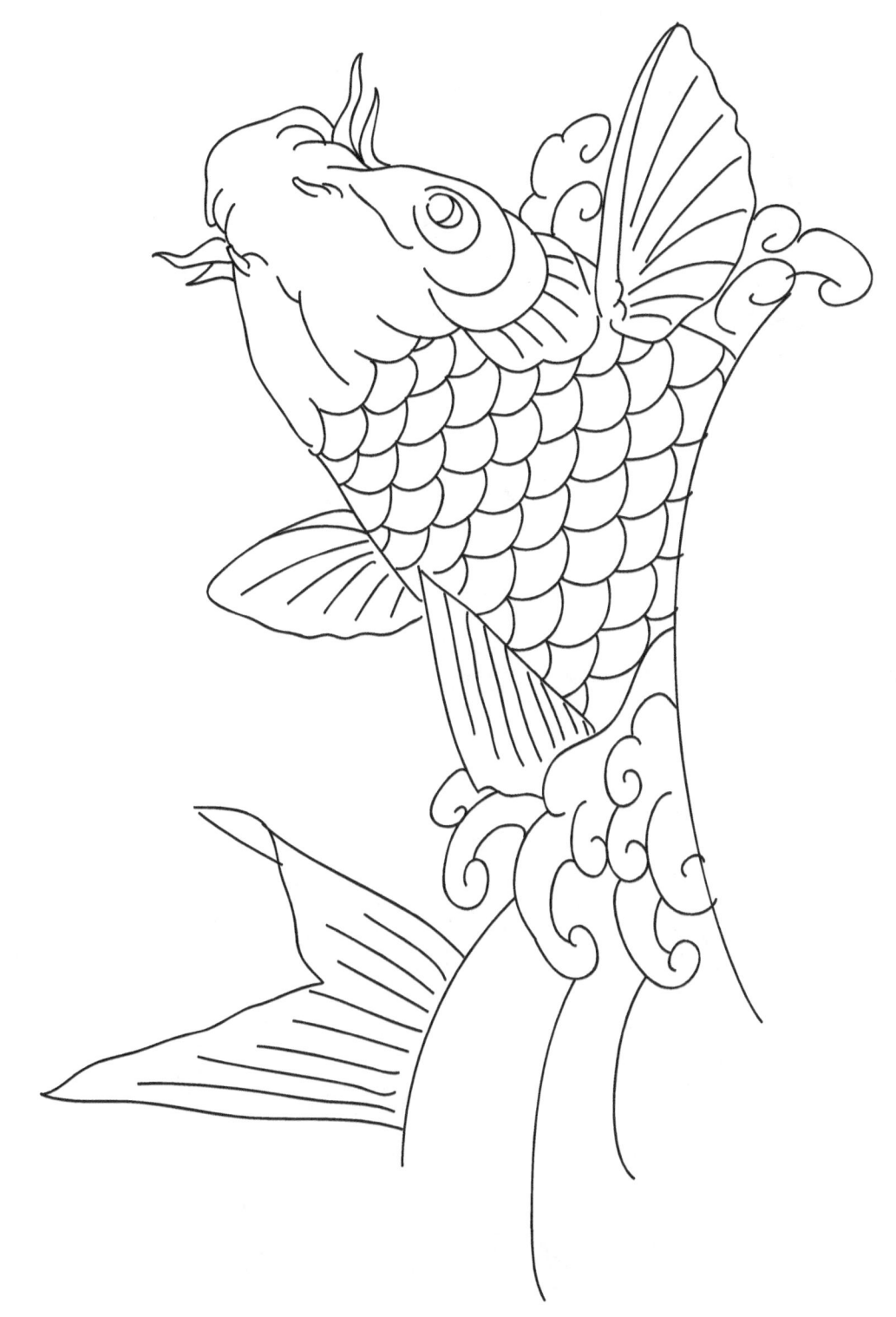

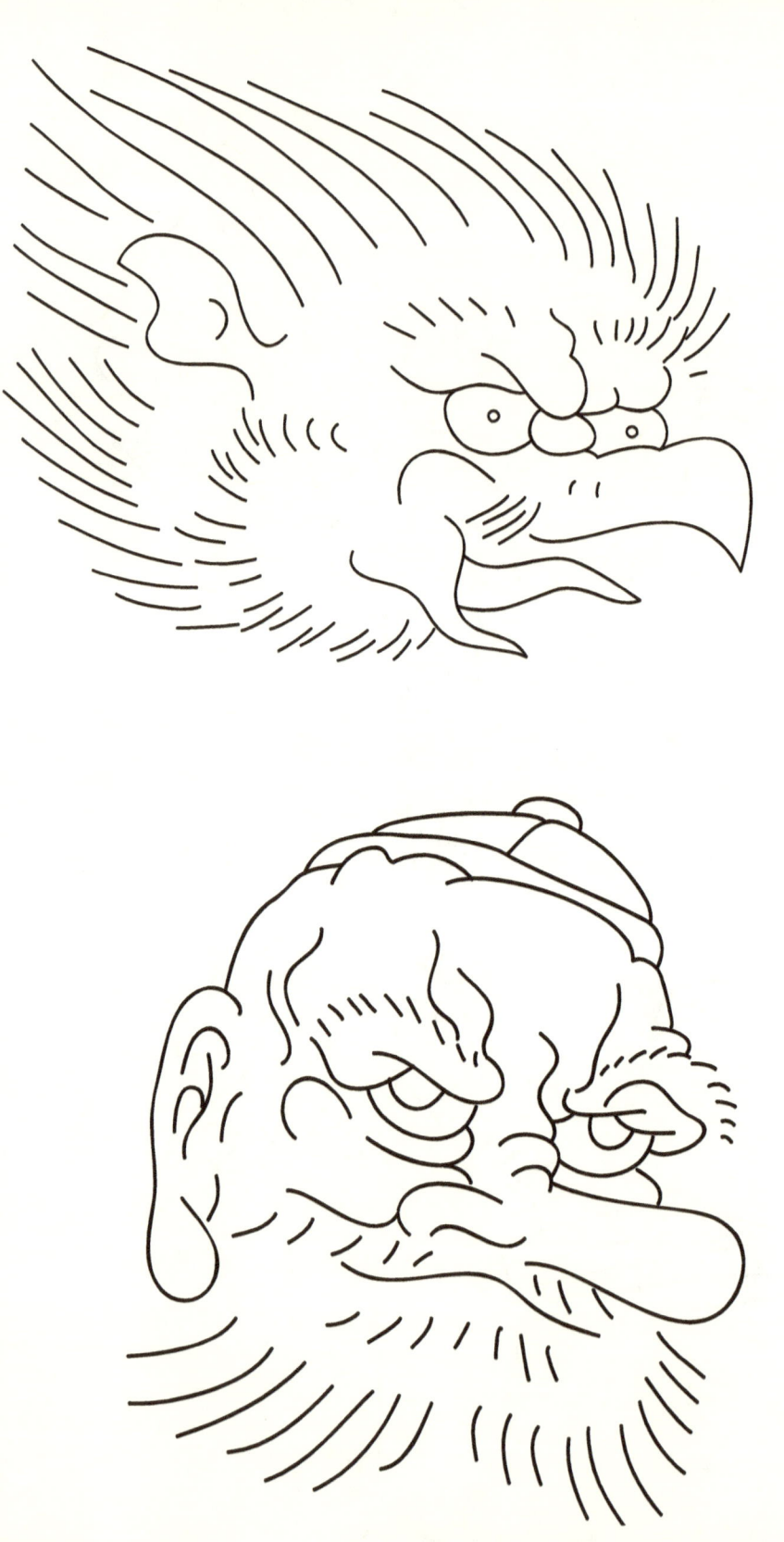

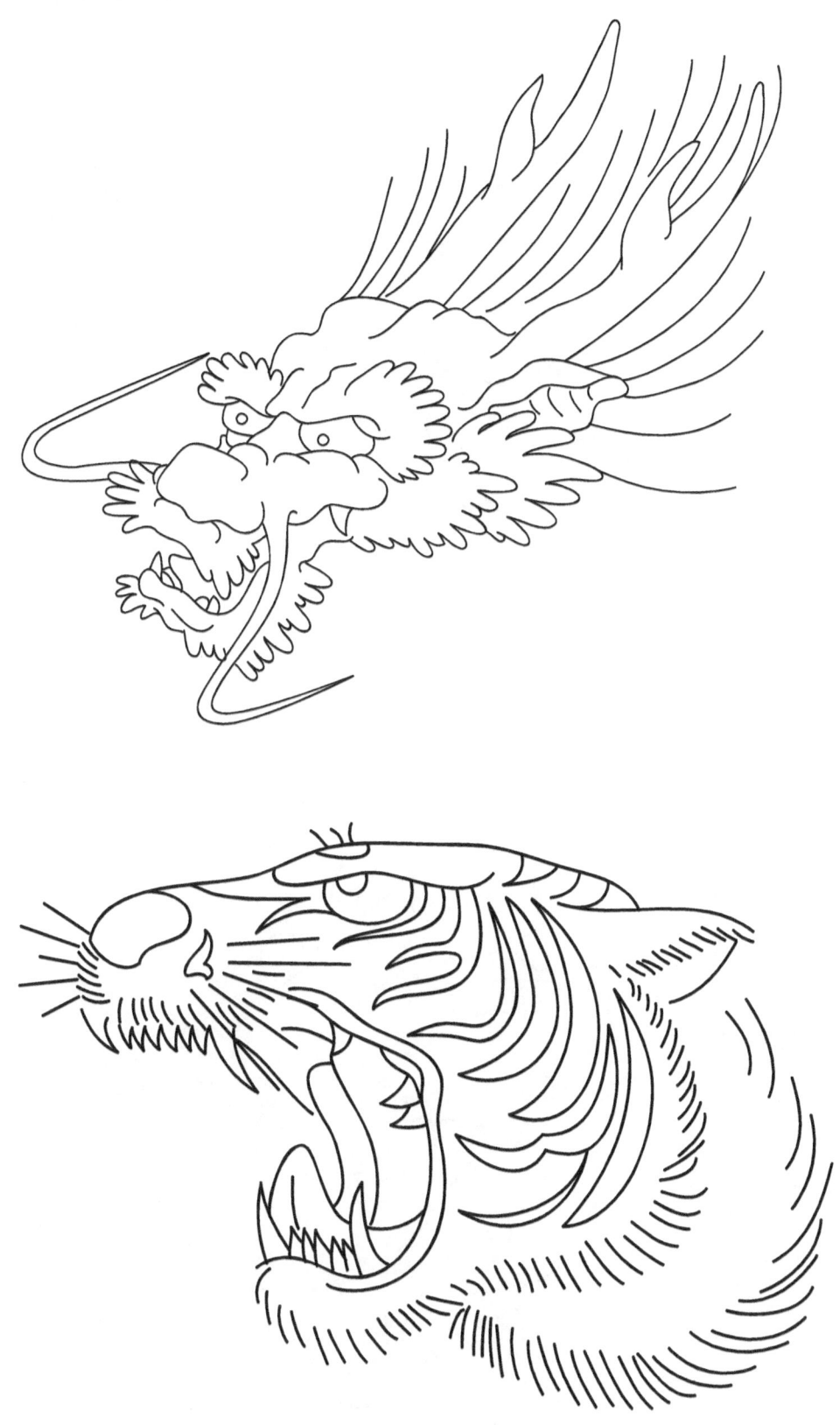

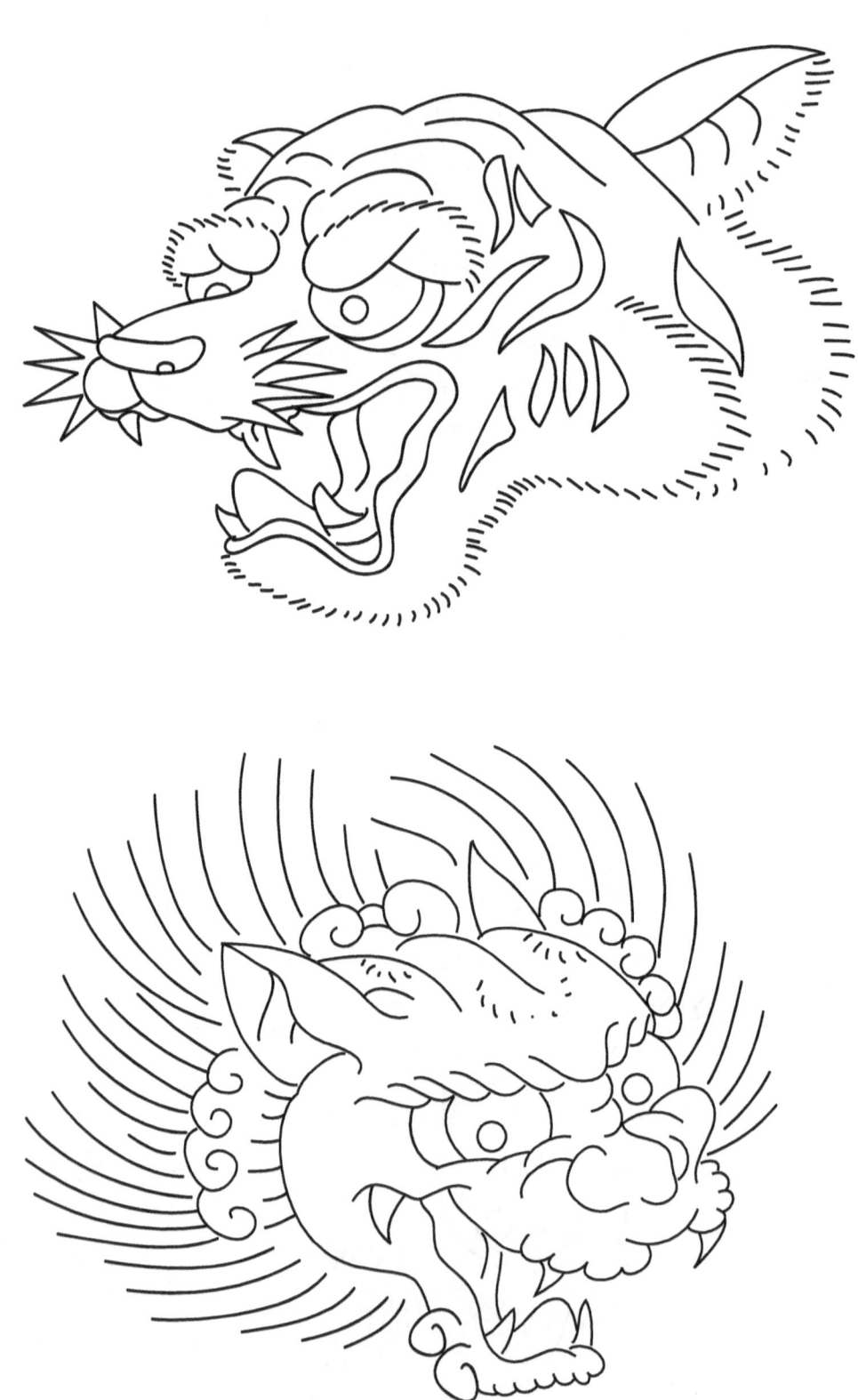

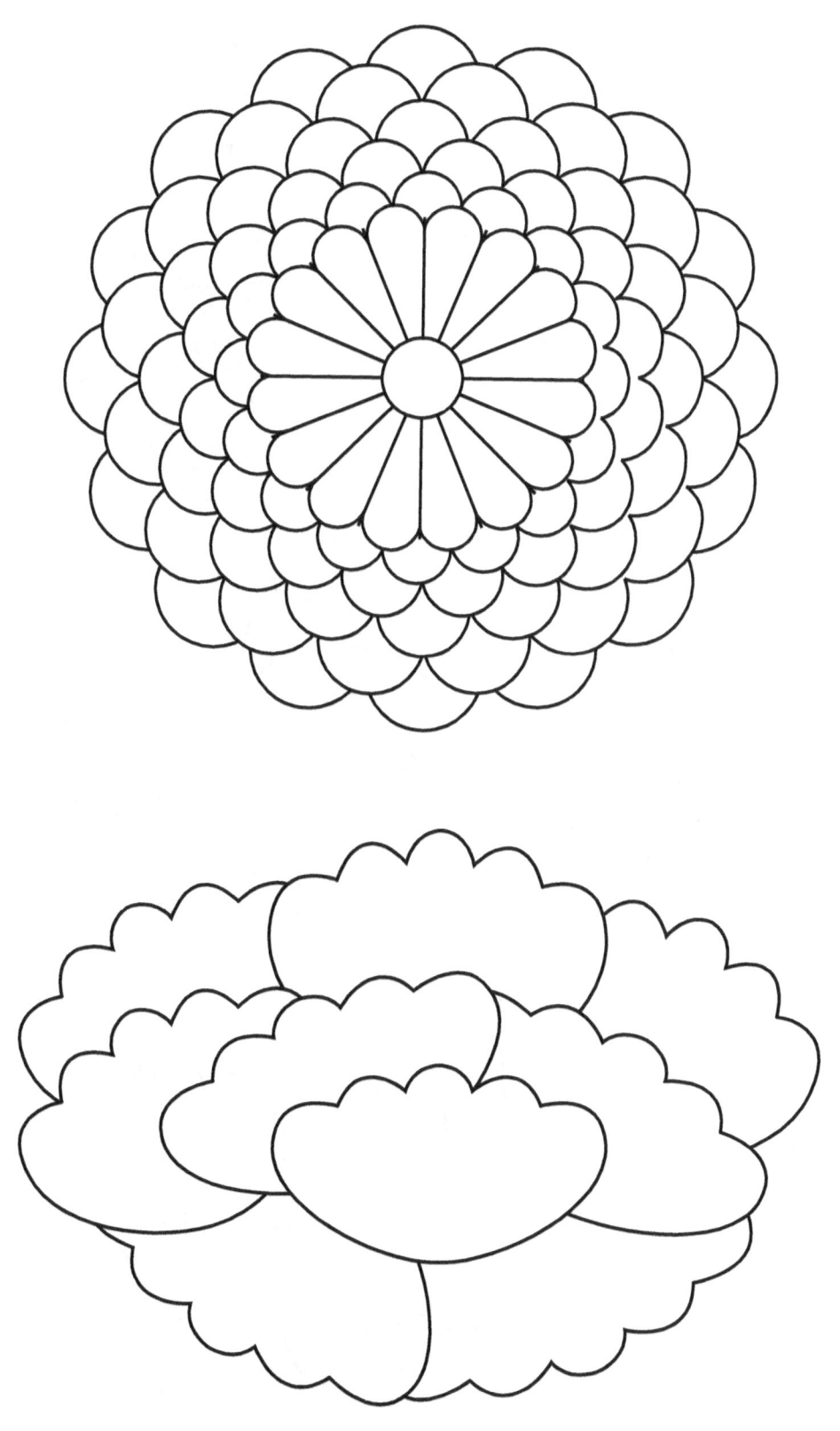

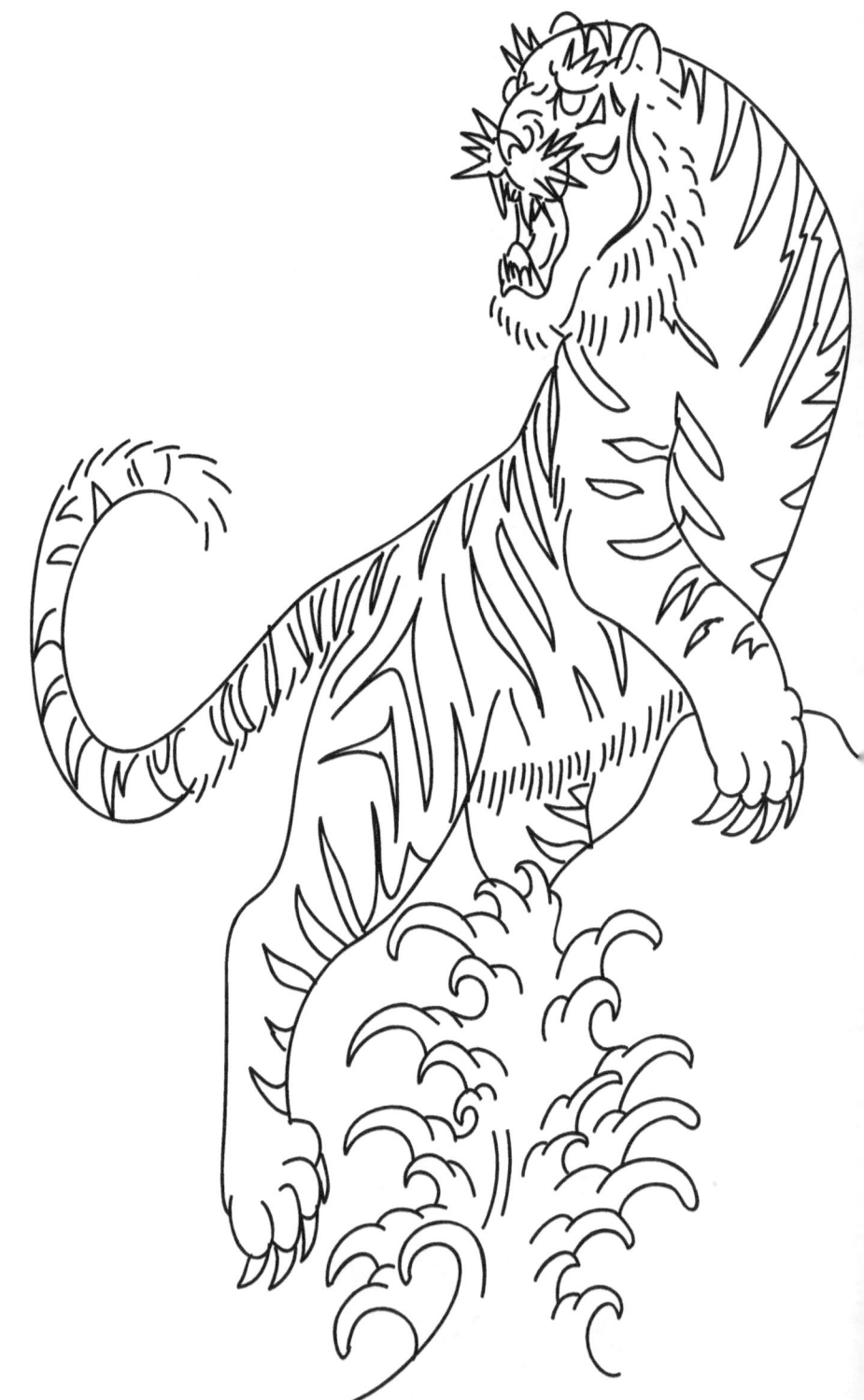

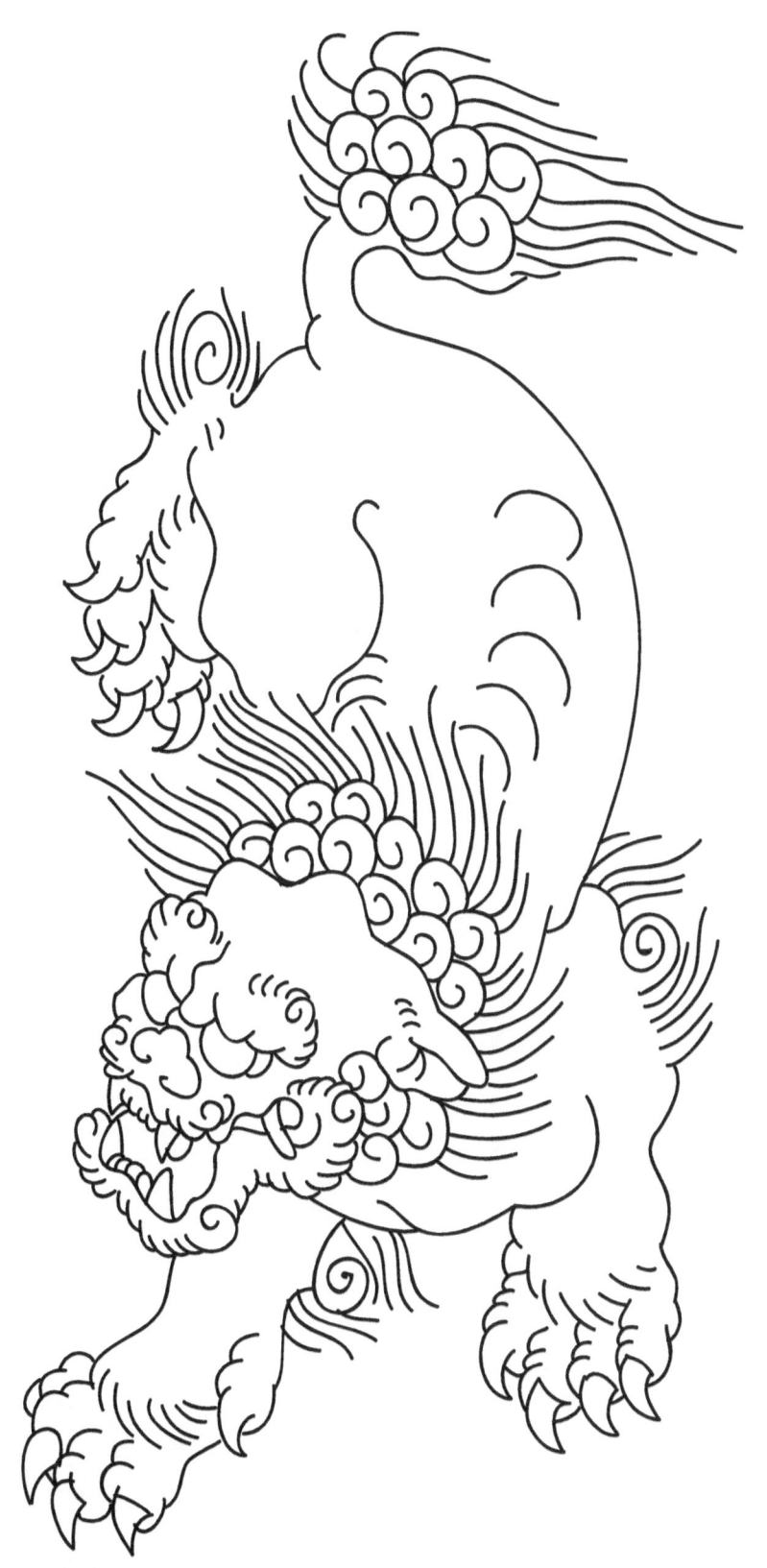

www.ingramcontent.com/pod-product-compliance
Lightning Source LLC
Chambersburg PA
CBHW030010190526
45157CB00015B/2170

* 9 7 8 1 1 0 5 9 9 9 3 5 2 *